I Worked on Spitfires

I Worked on Spitfires

The Memoirs of a Member of RAF Groundcrew and his Part in the Victory in Europe

Ron Chapman

AIR WORLD

First published in Great Britain in 2024
by Air World
An imprint of
Pen & Sword Books Limited
Yorkshire – Philadelphia

Copyright © Estate of Ronald L. Chapman, 2024
ISBN: 978-1-39905-726-4

The right of the late Ronald L. Chapman to be identified as Author of this work has been asserted by his estate in accordance with the Copyright, Designs and Patents Act 1988. A CIP catalogue record for this book is available from the British Library All rights reserved.

No part of this book may be reproduced or transmitted in any form or by any means, electronic or mechanical including photocopying, recording or by any information storage and retrieval system, without permission from the Publisher in writing.

Typeset in INDIA by IMPEC eSolutions
Printed and bound in the UK by CPI Group (UK) Ltd, Croydon, CR0 4YY

Pen & Sword Books Limited incorporates the imprints of Archaeology, Atlas, Aviation, Battleground, Digital, Discovery, Family History, Fiction, History, Local, Local History, Maritime, Military, Military Classics, Politics, Select, Transport, True Crime, After the Battle, Air World, Claymore Press, Frontline Publishing, Leo Cooper, Remember When, Seaforth Publishing, The Praetorian Press, Wharncliffe Books, Wharncliffe Local History, Wharncliffe Transport, Wharncliffe True Crime and White Owl.

For a complete list of Pen & Sword titles please contact:

PEN & SWORD BOOKS LIMITED
47 Church Street, Barnsley, South Yorkshire, S70 2AS, UK
E-mail: enquiries@pen-and-sword.co.uk
Website: www.pen-and-sword.co.uk

or

PEN AND SWORD BOOKS,
1950 Lawrence Road, Havertown, PA 19083, USA
E-mail: Uspen-and-sword@casematepublishers.com
Website: www.penandswordbooks.com

Contents

Foreword: 'The Auld Alliance'	vii
Preface	x
Imagination	xii
Introduction and Acknowledgements	xiii
Chapter 1 René Mouchotte	1
Chapter 2 *Les Forces Ariennes Francaise Libre*	5
Chapter 3 Dieppe	18
Chapter 4 A Boy from Islington	40
Chapter 5 2nd Tactical Air Force	114
Chapter 6 D-Day	123
Chapter 7 Menin – Wevelgem	139
Chapter 8 Duerne near Antwerp (The Hell Hole)	156
Chapter 9 England Ahead (Fairwood Common)	180
Chapter 10 Back to the Fighting	193
Chapter 11 Fassberg	202
Chapter 12 Simone at Blankenberge	208
Chapter 13 Back to the Squadron	218
Appendix: Lost Companions	225

Foreword

'The Auld Alliance'

I feel that it is a tremendous privilege to be invited by the author of this fascinating book to write a foreword.

I happened to be commanding the R.A.F. Station at Turnhouse at the time the Free French Squadron was formed so I was fortunate enough to get to know many of the pilots and ground crews there, and later, when I was appointed to relieve that great fighter pilot Group Captain 'Sailor' Malan late in 1944 as C.O. of 145 Wing I found many well-known faces once again.

At that time 145 Wing consisted of one British and four French squadrons. The four French squadrons were Cigones, Alsace, Ile de France, and Cigone (Berry). The British squadron was No 74 R.A.F. I believe that probably all the French fighter pilots in Europe at that time were in this Wing and what a magnificent bunch of people they all were.

The story tells us much about the people, the places, the work, the play, the joys, the sorrows, the fear, the gallantry, the misery, the comradeship and all those other things that go to make up what happens in war.

The author has obviously spent countless hours in researching and thousands of miles in travelling in order to tell us what really happened, and he makes it quite plain that all of us who love our countries and freedom owe a tremendous debt to our French colleagues.

For me personally, I have nothing but admiration and affection for all those pilots and ground crews, French and English of all the squadrons in 145 Wing which I was privileged to command.

Group Captain Loel Guinness OBE
Commanding Officer No.145 Free French Wing
2nd Tactical Air Force RAF

Scottish folklore tells the story of how the French and the Scots became friends.

At the time of the Saxon (North German) invasions of England and France in about the fifth century, the Scots who were always at war with the Anglo Saxons, and the French who were always at war with the Saxons, formed an alliance against their mutual enemy.

They went to each other's aid in battle and supported the preservation of Christianity, at the same time exchanging methods of education and culture.

From that time, the Scottish Standard (flag) which is a Red Lion rampant upon a yellow background, was surrounded by the Fleur de Lys emblem of France. This meant to show the fierce Lion of Scotland in partnership with the gentleness of the Lilies of France and to symbolise the friendship of the nations forever.

Up until the time of James, the Scottish King who became James I of England thus uniting the British Isles in 1603 and forming the beginning of the United Kingdom, the French and the Scots were always ready to aid each other against English invasion.

French and Scottish nobility frequently intermarried and gave shelter to each other in times of persecution (Bonny [*sic*] Prince Charlie and Mary Queen of Scots).

During the Second World War when the French pilots escaped to prove their allegiance to [General Charles] de Gaulle, it was in Scotland that they formed their first Free French Fighting Squadron, thereby continuing the 'Auld Alliance'.

Gilroi Simeon, 1990

Preface

I was delighted to be asked to write the preface for *I Worked on Spitfires*, though, of course, I never met Ron Chapman. However, I did meet his son, Mark, in 2011.

In 2007 I sponsored the name of Squadron Leader René Mouchotte on the Battle of Britain Memorial Wall at Capel-le-Ferne near Folkestone and, through my website, was appealing for any help I could get with research. Mark Chapman responded, telling me that his father, Ron, had great respect for René, having believed him to be strict, but fair and generous. We had to meet – and meet we did at Marlow in Buckinghamshire.

The meeting was pleasant and fruitful. Mark arrived with a small lapel badge from the Aero Club Jean Mermoz, to which René had belonged in 1936. This had been given to Ron by René's mother when the pair met in France many years after the war. Mark also brought with him a copy of an unpublished book his father had written in the 1980s. It was typed on A4 paper and mounted in a looseleaf binding folder. Mark generously gave me the copy but not the lapel badge. (Years later I was to be given one by René's family). Reading the book, I was introduced to another side of the war, that of the ground crews who kept the planes in the sky. Theirs was an incredibly arduous task involving hugely long working hours in the most awful conditions. They too suffered death and privation.

Their work conditions at home, and more so when their units moved to the Continent, were appalling – dreadful food, insanitary conditions, lumpy beds and often just the floor on which to sleep and sometimes no sleep at all as they worked through the nights to keep the planes airworthy and armed. There was the constant fear of enemy aircraft attacking airfields, and the V1 and V2 rockets which dropped from the sky and exploded, bringing death and destruction.

I felt the book was worthy of publication, but was powerless to do anything to help until 2022.

René Mouchotte, killed in 1943, wrote personal diaries during the war. Afterwards, in 1949, his diaries were posthumously published in French. He was a renowned, respected and loved commander here in the UK and his diaries were re-published in English in 1956. I wanted to have them re-published.

Fate is a strange beast. Dilip Sarkar, a prolific writer and expert on the Battle of Britain, visited Capel-le-Ferne and my name was mentioned. Dilip contacted me and, to cut a long story short, he facilitated having *The Mouchotte Diaries* republished by Pen and Sword in November 2022 under the title *Free French Spitfire Hero* with additional explanatory notes from Dilip and my 'search' as the Epilogue.

Mark Chapman and I had remained in touch, and I saw a possibility for him. Having recommended Ron Chapman's story to an editor at Pen and Sword, I am absolutely thrilled that his book is to be published – albeit forty-three years later than he wished.

Reading the proofs, I couldn't put the story down and finished it in five hours. I hope you enjoy this look 'behind the scenes', as it were, of the brave men who kept the 'planes and pilots in the air during the Second World War, without whom …

Jan Leeming, 2024

Imagination

I walked on hallowed ground today imagined I could hear
A squadron of Spitfires taking off without a trace of fear
An early morning sortie a sky full of planes
Watch them returning some to land others to crash in flames

All were young men with hopes and their dreams
Destined to die for a cause, such a waste it all now seems
Day after day the battle ensued always looking into the sun
Flying in tight formation until they meet the dreaded Hun

To us on the ground we waited, we prayed
As we saw then returning such courage they had displayed
Always someone missing, always someone dead
Like the loose pages in a book always unread

I walked on hallowed ground today
Remembering friends of mine
For those who gave their lives, never forget
This was their moment in time.

Ronald L. Chapman,
4 September 1979

Introduction and Acknowledgements

The basis for this true story began many years ago after reading numerous books written by former wartime pilots with the RAF Fighter Command, which retold the many events that took place in aerial combat over Great Britain and Europe during the period 1939-1945 of the Second World War. The writers of these books were of various nationalities, and I was always surprised to find that very little had been written in Great Britain about the *Forces Aériennes Françaises Libres* – the FAFL (Free French air forces).

This then, was the dilemma in which I found myself; after searching libraries throughout the country for any reference to the men of France who escaped in large numbers from all parts of their country, including those Frenchmen who succeeded in reaching Great Britain from as far away as French Canada and the French Colonies. The methods of escape and transportation from France to England, often via Gibraltar, for many of these patriots of France, are in principle too numerous to recount in this book. However, it is my intention to outline a small selection of them.

For the readers who may find it unusual for an Englishman to concern himself with the Free French fighter squadrons and the pilots, who were formed and based in Great Britain in the early years of the Second World War, may I simply explain that

I served, not as a pilot, but as a member of the British ground crews, a unique band of men, seconded to the squadrons from all parts of this country, who lived, worked and died during the Second World War, servicing the fighter aircraft that the French pilots flew in combat, day after day, against the fighter pilots and aces of the German Luftwaffe.

As I began my research into the FAFL, I found that my first breakthrough came by chance when a copy of a book entitled, *The Mouchotte Diaries* came into my possession. This book had been translated from French into English and was edited by André Dezarrois, a friend of René Mouchotte and his family. Published in France after the war under the title *Les Carnets de René Mouchotte*, it was first published in Great Britain in 1956, by Staples Press Ltd.

That story of the late Commandant René Mouchotte's escape to England, along with several other French pilots, is by itself quite dramatic. Such was the respect in which he was held by his fellow countrymen and by the French, British and Allied pilots who flew with him in combat against the Luftwaffe that it is an understatement to say, that the RAF lost a great friend and aerial tactician by his strange and untimely death in the autumn of 1943.

In November 1941, under the command of Commandant Philippe de Scitivaux, Mouchotte became a flight commander of the first Free French squadron of Spitfires, named the 'Ile de France'. No. 341 Squadron was formed and based at Turnhouse in Edinburgh. A year later, in January 1943, Mouchotte was promoted to command No. 341 'Alsace' Squadron, the second of the Free French squadrons, and he remained as the commanding officer until his death, later that year.

Introduction and Acknowledgements   xv

Before I begin the story of the French pilots and my involvement with No. 341 Squadron during the war, it would be completely unfair to the memory of André Dezarrois, if I did not acknowledge a quotation from his book, *The Mouchotte Diaries* in which he writes: 'Let us hope that one day a larger edition of this sober, simply-written book, quick with the memory of the dead, will complete the history of the "Ile de France" Squadron.' [This is indeed the case, as Mouchotte's diaries were republished in 2022 with additional material by Air World under the title *Free French Spitfire Hero: The Diaries of and Search For René Mouchotte*, complied by Dilip Sarkar and Jan Leeming – Ed.]

André Dezarrois goes on to say that two men could have completed the story of their leader, René Mouchotte, for whom they grieved, ('Alsace' too, awaits its chronicler) but they, his followers, are also dead: Commandant Schloesing, killed in a tragic accident and Commandant Christian Martel killed in action.

Recently, I returned to my beloved Belgium, where in conversation with the former commanding officer of No. 350 Squadron (Belgium), General Baron Michel Donnet, I outlined this story. General Donnet, who also escaped from Belgium in 1940, knew and flew as a young RAF pilot in Great Britain, with many of the French pilots on British squadrons. His strongest comment was that this story should be written, as he put it, 'For the generations to come'.

It goes without saying, that I could not hope to achieve this mammoth task without a great deal of encouragement and assistance. The list is endless; however, I must express my sincere thanks to the following:

Madame de Tedesco, widow of the late Count Jean de Tedesco, former Free French pilot with No. 340 Squadron.
André Moynet, former pilot with No. 340 Squadron.
Henri Lafont, former pilot with No. 341 Squadron and one of the original escapees with Mouchotte in 1940.
Group Captain Loel Guinness, the former CO at Turnhouse aerodrome, Edinburgh and friend to the French pilots. He subsequently took command of all the Free French wing of the 2nd Tactical Air Force in late 1944, taking over from the late Group Captain 'Sailor' Malan of South Africa, our CO, prior to and after the 'D-Day' landings in Normandy.
Carlo Van Troostenberghe of Middelkerke, Belgium.
Mrs Helen Archibald of Edinburgh.
Alan Knott, former Sergeant Armourer and member of the ground staff with the French squadrons.

I apologise to the many former Free French pilots that I have not named and to the wartime establishments that I have been unable to trace or contact.

Chapter 1

René Mouchotte

In May of 1940, when the French Government capitulated to the German attacks, many of the pilots of the French Air Force who had survived the air battles, made the decision to escape to England, in the hope that they could continue the fight against the Luftwaffe.

At the beginning the number of pilots attempting to escape was quite small but over the ensuing months it gradually became obvious that these young sons of France found many unique forms of transportation, in their determination to reach the RAF in England.

Not all the escapees came from France. Many took up the call and travelled vast distances from as far away as French Canada, the Belgian Congo and the numerous French Colonies throughout the world. Of the young men who made the attempt to escape from France or its colonies, those who were successful found that they were immediately outlawed by the French Government and were condemned to death in their absence.

Although many attempts to escape were extremely precarious, a large number were highly successful, enabling these young pilots to reach Gibraltar and then to England and the RAF. Tragically, many of the so-called escapees were either captured and imprisoned or died en route in their attempt to reach freedom.

It was during my research that some remarkable stories of escape came to light and while it is not my intention to revive sad memories for the families of French pilots killed in combat or flying accidents, during that period of the war, I feel that these tales should be told to pay tribute and draw attention to those young patriots who gave their lives for the people of Great Britain and the many subjugated people of Europe, regardless of nationality, colour or creed. As the late General de Gaulle once said, to an audience, when visiting the French squadrons on an English airfield: 'France is France!'

With the cessation of hostilities of the Second World War, the true story concerning the death of René Mouchotte, was revealed to his mother and family and his personal diaries came to light. It was following the receipt of the diaries and his personal effects that Madame Mouchotte lent them to a family friend, André Dezarrois, who requested that he publish the diaries as an example to the young men of France.

André Dezarrois was a former fighter pilot himself. Before the Second World War he had been a member of Guynemer's Wing – 'The Cigognes' – the famous French squadron, which during the last war, became No. 329 (GC I/2 'Cicognes') Squadron RAF.

When one of France's greatest leaders of the resistance was asked by André Dezarrois, whether the diary should be published he gave the following reply: 'The diaries are not "literature". They contain love of country, the heart of a fighter pilot, a leader's soul. The sons of France need the nourishment they have to give.'

Following that statement, I can only add that in the course of my research, carried out over many years, it is clear that the late Commandant René Mouchotte's story has become a legend to the classes of young officers joining the French Air Force in the post-war years.

The news of the capitulation of France soon became known worldwide and left many French servicemen wondering which direction to take. In Oran, North Africa, a large fleet of aircraft and numerous pilots were grounded on the orders of the French Government. Nevertheless, several attempts to escape in the grounded aircraft were made by experienced pilots, following the signing of an armistice by France. Gibraltar was the first base they made for in their break for freedom to England. The French authorities in Oran, being aware of these attempts to escape, forbad any form of flying and imposed a curfew on all pilots stationed there.

Three pilots had already escaped, followed by another attempt when two men stole a small plane and took off for Gibraltar. Several further endeavours to get away by air ended in disaster because the aircraft had been put out of action by the authorities. Some efforts by determined pilots using stolen planes which had been sabotaged by mechanics, ended in crashes on take-off.

It was during this period that Mouchotte, along with his close friends, Charles Guerin, Henri Lafont, Sorret and several others, made the decision to steal an aircraft and head for Gibraltar. They were successful although the operation was not without very dangerous and hair-raising moments.

The most precarious was when, having taken off with the heavily loaded aircraft, Mouchotte discovered, on checking the propeller pitch, that there was little change on the rev-counter. On closer inspection it was revealed that the mechanics had altered the pitch of the propeller to a coarse pitch. It was only due to Mouchotte's flying ability that this group of escapees were successful in arriving safely in Gibraltar.

Emile Fayolle, a friend of Mouchotte, also made his way to England to join the RAF and became a member of the Free French Air Force.

Featuring throughout this account is the close association between the French squadrons and Scotland, not merely in terms of geography but between the French pilots, the British ground crews serving with them and the ladies of the country.

It is not my task to write their individual stories in this book, however, the men of France seemed destined to repeat history and become entwined with Scotland. There are many happy and a few sad tales that could be told of the unions between the men of the French squadrons and the young 'lassies' of Scotland, who met and fell in love during 1941-1943 in the districts around the airfields of Ayr, Drem and Turnhouse.

Chapter 2

Les Forces Ariennes Francaise Libre

French pilots who successfully reached the RAF in England, found that they were required to pass through RAF training units irrespective of past flying experience. Having qualified, they were posted to various RAF Hurricane squadrons, throughout Great Britain.

In accordance with this arrangement, René Mouchotte found he was separated from Charles Guerin and de Labouchère, who had escaped with him from North Africa. Also on the strength of the Hurricane squadrons were a number of Polish and Czech pilots trying to convert to the Hurricane fighter, sometimes with tragic results.

French pilots based on RAF Squadrons in Northern Ireland found that their presence caused a certain amount of newspaper interest, so there was a requirement for them to be on their best behaviour. Other French pilots were promoted to RAF non-commissioned ranks and were posted to Polish squadrons based at Northolt on the outskirts of London. It was at this station that more accidents happened, not always fatal, but enough to establish the difficulties of adapting to Hurricanes after French aircraft.

At the same time the pilots discovered that the German Messerschmitt 109s were much faster than the Hurricane in aerial combat. Another danger for those based in and around the capital, was that when returning to their bases, they had great difficulty in navigating between the profusion of barrage balloons surrounding London. This often resulted in a fatal crash.

During January 1941, No. 615 Squadron (known as 'Churchill's Own') already containing several French pilots including René Mouchotte, was posted from the Scottish base to Kenley aerodrome, near Croydon on the outskirts of London. It was whilst the squadron was based at Kenley that Charles Guerin and Henri Lafont joined Mouchotte and their comrades on 615.

It was during this period that an order was issued that French, Polish and Czech pilots were not to take part in any low-level raids over France. As outlawed nationals of their respective countries, they could be executed if forced or shot down over France and taken prisoner by the Germans.

While 615 Squadron was still at Kenley, Mouchotte was commissioned to the rank of pilot officer (*sous lieutenant*, French rank). Shortly after his promotion, several English pilots on 615 were shot down, amongst them, Mouchotte's flight commander, Foxley-Norris – at the time of writing, Air Chief Marshal Sir Christopher Foxley-Norris – who fortunately baled-out and although battered and bruised, returned to the squadron the same day.

Whilst being sent on a rest from operations, Mouchotte spent some time in and around Beaconsfield, a country town in Buckinghamshire. It was there that Mouchotte met a French pilot who had sustained a broken arm at a training school in England. He had escaped from France in 1940 and had managed to contact his mother before leaving, only to learn that his three brothers had been killed fighting the Germans, his two sisters, both nurses, had also been killed and his father was a prisoner in Germany. Listening to this sad story, Mouchotte promised to try and get him a posting to 615 Squadron, so that he could join his French colleagues in avenging his family.

During April 1941, the squadron and flight commanders of 615 were absent from operations at Kenley and, from over twenty French pilots, Mouchotte was selected and appointed acting squadron leader of 615. Towards the end of the month, the entire squadron was posted to RAF Valley in Wales, where flying operations were confined to patrolling over convoys at sea.

Early in May, a tragic incident took place on an operation over the sea, which Mouchotte was never to overcome. The squadron had been airborne on convoy duty for about an hour, when Mouchotte noticed a white cloud emitting from the engine of the plane flown by Charles Guerin. Not only was Guerin Mouchotte's best friend but he was also one of the original escapees with him on the flight from Algeria to Gibraltar in 1940. The plane crashed into the sea at approximately fifty feet and despite a search by ships from the convoy and aircraft from 615, Charles Guerin was never found.

A few days later, on a similar operation, Mouchotte witnessed another grim loss when Briere, whose plane also developed engine failure over the sea, crashed without trace. From the original group of Frenchmen stationed at Kenley, only Henri Lafont and Mouchotte were still alive. Following these personal tragedies, Mouchotte joined the No. 601 'City of London' Squadron and was decorated with the *Croix de Guerre*.

A young French-Canadian pilot from 601, tried to land when his aircraft developed engine trouble over the sea, but crashed on the beach and he was drowned in shallow water.

Sometime later, the RAF took the unprecedented step of choosing to appoint a Frenchman, René Mouchotte, as a flight commander of 601 Squadron and he was promoted to the rank of flight lieutenant. There was also news that the formation of an all Free French Squadron was possible in the coming months.

Two more French pilots from 615 were killed: Garnier was attacked by a Messerschmitt 110 and shot down, whilst the French-Canadian, Albert Boulanger, returning to base after a sortie, was attempting to land, when the petrol tank of his aircraft caught fire and he crashed to the ground at full speed.

In August, Mouchotte's squadron was posted to Manston in Kent, another south coast fighter aerodrome, where he met more French pilots including Captain Philippe de Scitivaux, Bernard Duperier and François de Labouchère, already stationed there. At this time, it is important to point out that because the Free French pilots had families still living in towns throughout France, they chose to use English or French-Canadian names, hoping to safeguard their relatives from the possibility of intimidation by the Germans or revenge if the pilots were unfortunate enough to get shot down over France during an operation.

Mouchotte may have had a premonition in 1943 in which he sensed his ultimate destiny. Alternatively, it may have been the result of the tremendous friendship he enjoyed in the company of French-Canadian colleagues; in either event he chose to adopt a Canadian name as his *nom de guerre* and acquired a Canadian accent and a Canadian flash on the shoulder of his uniform.

In the middle of October 1941, the much talked of formation of an all French fighter squadron became a reality, when on a visit to the Hornchurch aerodrome in Essex, Mouchotte was taken to meet the great man himself, General Charles de Gaulle, who was on a visit to meet the French pilots. It was whilst Mouchotte and the other pilots were at Hornchurch that the official statement was released to the effect that they were to move to Turnhouse aerodrome on the outskirts of Edinburgh to form the first Free French Spitfire squadron in Great Britain; to be called No. 340 (Ile de France) Squadron RAF. This consisted of two flights – 'A' Flight ('Paris') and 'B' Flight ('Versailles').

During November 1941, the squadron was formed at Turnhouse and was initially commanded by an English squadron leader. Of the two flight commanders, Captain de Scitivaux became the commanding officer of 'A' Flight with Mouchotte as his second in command. 'B' Flight was led by Captain Bernard Duperier with Emile Fayolle as his second in command.

The tragic news reached Turnhouse of the death of Captain Laurent who was returning from an operation to his base in the south of England. The low-lying mist and fog, surrounding the area, blinded him and he crashed into a hill.

During their stay in Scotland, not only at Turnhouse but at Drem and Ayr, the French became very attached to the Scottish towns and to Edinburgh in particular. The off-duty pilots and ground crews caused a sensation in their elegant dark blue uniforms with gold adornments, standing out in contrast to the British on the nightly excursions into the towns. For some young ladies from Edinburgh, who met and eventually married these young men, the consequences were beyond imagination.

In early December 1941, several Free French pilots arrived from the south to join 340 at Turnhouse; these included Lieutenant Claude, Sous Lieutenant Fournier, Sergeant Demas, Lieutenant Gilbert, Sous Chef Debec, Sous Chef Daoulas, Capitaine Bechoff, Lieutenant Chavin and Sergeant Taconet. At this time news reached Great Britain of Japan's attack on Pearl Harbor, where the American battle fleet had been anchored. The 7 December 1941 became an infamous date in the annals of naval history and brought America, the bastion of freedom during the First World War, once again into the conflict of the second global conflict. The news of America's declaration of war, not only against Japan but the Germans, set the telephone wires buzzing across the world with the obvious connotations for all the nations involved in the monstrous war.

With the coming of 1942, the establishment of the ground crews on the No. 340 (Free French) Squadron was enlarged by a number of British RAF ground crews, joining the squadron to supplement the French ground crews already at Turnhouse.

The British crews were made up of various trades and comprised aircraft fitters, riggers, armourers, instrument bashers and motor transport drivers. All the crews were already trained and highly skilled in the craft of maintaining and servicing Spitfires. A large proportion of this unusual band of men were from all parts of Scotland, whilst the rest of these experienced, operational crews, were made up of men from Yorkshire, Lancashire and the North East, mixed with Londoners, Irishmen, Welshmen and various other parts of England. This good mix of men proved to be extremely loyal, not only to their French pilots and the aircraft but to their own particular trade. *Esprit de corps* was at its highest level.

As I have already mentioned, many romantic associations blossomed between the men at Turnhouse or Drem and the young ladies in the district. In a number of cases, marriage became the order of the day, thus reaffirming the link between the Scots and the French in the years that followed to the end of the war and after. The re-birth of the 'Auld Alliance', founded a few hundred years previously, once more asserted itself and forged the union.

It is only fair to state that serving with the Free French was a group of Canadian and French-Canadian men who had travelled vast distances from their homelands in Canada and North America to Europe in order to volunteer for service with the RAF.

After the collapse of France in June 1940, their dilemma was such, that a great many of them, feeling that all was lost, resolved to return to their homes. It was to their lasting credit that they stayed on in England, having been persuaded at the highest level, that the fight would continue.

Their merit was confirmed in the years that followed as they displayed such bravery and dedication to the task of defeating the German Luftwaffe. One French-Canadian friend, finding himself in hospital in Belgium with me, explained their philosophy regarding France: Montreal after Paris, was the largest city in France, followed by the cities of Québec and Marseille; an explanation I have never forgotten.

In the New Year of 1942, the 'Ile de France' and its French pilots received a lot of publicity, and the aerodrome was continually invaded by journalists and newspaper reporters. In February 1942, an article appeared in *The Scotsman* newspaper, published in Edinburgh, concerning the Free French Spitfire Squadron based in Scotland. A banner photograph appeared showing the pilots who had been scrambled, running to their Spitfires, lined up on dispersal points. The squadron letters of GW, identifying No. 340 'Ile de France' can be seen clearly on the fuselage of the aircraft.

Below the photograph was the story of another Free French pilot, already the holder of the *Croix de Guerre* for bravery in the air whilst fighting the Luftwaffe in France. He had escaped from an airfield in Algiers by taking off in an aircraft, which was fortunately fuelled and serviced. He took off in a cloud of dust and headed in the direction of the Mediterranean, chased by two flights of fighters loyal to the Vichy Government. He eventually eluded his pursuers and made for Gibraltar, where he landed safely. Jumping from his aircraft he offered his services to the Free French and to the RAF Officer who greeted him. This pilot was one of those from the 'Ile de France' Squadron featured in the newspaper article.

Another pilot on the squadron had been in hospital with a broken arm in 1940. When he received information that the German Army was closing in on the town, he jumped from his bed and ran to the harbour, where he managed to find a boat and crew. He requisitioned the vessel and procured enough coal to enable the crew to sail the boat out of port, just as the

Germans entered the town. The crowded boat docked safely in England.

Three more pilots had fled from their country, three days after the German occupation of Paris. They drove a car through the capital and onto a military aerodrome, where they stole three aircraft from a hangar, started the engines and took off. As they flew over the rooftops of Paris, they were attacked by heavy German gunfire but all three escaped and headed for Bordeaux where they believed they would be safe.

On landing at the aerodrome, they found that instead of congratulations, they were all arrested by the Vichy authorities and imprisoned. The aircraft were, of course, confiscated by officials of the Government. However, they effected an escape from prison and stole a German, field grey, staff car in which they drove out onto a road, just as a German convoy was passing. They were suddenly overtaken by other German staff cars, also painted field grey. Jammed in the middle of the convoy, unnoticed, the pilots discovered they were heading for unoccupied France. Having arrived at their destination without being challenged, they were able to escape to England.

More publicity followed the French squadron when a news film was organised, featuring pilots scrambling from the Scottish aerodrome for the benefit of the local newsmen. The intention had been that after take-off, the pilots would fly in formation and execute the Cross of Lorraine in the sky over Scotland. Sadly, the weather changed, and the exercise was cancelled, much to the disappointment of the newsmen and photographers.

Early in February 1942, Captain Philippe de Scitivaux was promoted to the rank of commandant and took command of No. 340 'Ile de France' Squadron. This event was overshadowed by the occurrence of the squadron's first tragedy on the Scottish aerodrome. A young French pilot arriving fresh from training school, crashed when he attempted to land on the airfield.

With the news of the possibility of a visit by General de Gaulle to the 'Paris Squadron' (Ile de France), Mouchotte as commanding officer of 'A' Flight, arranged for the squadron's Spitfires to be painted and a small Cross of Lorraine was emblazoned on each aircraft, near to the cockpit. Mouchotte allocated another task to a Free French pilot with artistic flair; aristocrat Lieutenant Count Jean de Tedesco was asked to decorate the pilots' room in readiness for the great man's visit.

I will relate his personal and brief story which has a happy beginning but tragically sad ending. Lieutenant de Tedesco was a highly respected man and an excellent pilot and had shot down several German planes. During his posting to Scotland, he met and fell in love with a young lady from Edinburgh, whom he married. Later in the year, when the squadron was stationed at the famous Tangmere aerodrome, some 3 miles from the ancient and beautiful cathedral town of Chichester, in Sussex, Lieutenant de Tedesco was joined by his beautiful Scottish wife. Their marriage was eventually blessed with a son, born at the hospital in Chichester.

It followed that Lieutenant de Tedesco was posted from the 'Ile de France' Squadron to another Free French squadron that had been formed and sent out to help the Russian Air

Force. Sadly, he never returned for he was killed fighting the Luftwaffe over Russia in July 1943.

Countess de Tedesco, his widow, returned to her native Edinburgh where she raised her young son, who married whilst still a young student. Tragedy struck again when he died at an early age leaving a widow and small children, living in an area of Toronto in Canada. Count Jean de Tedesco's mother died soon after the end of the war, followed by the early death of his brother, in France.

It was purely by chance that I heard of this poignant story concerning our brave young Free French pilot of No. 340 'Ile de France' Squadron. When I had the honour and pleasure to talk to the charming and beautiful Madame de Tedesco, she gave me her permission to include this extract from her memory of Lieutenant Count de Tedesco, with whom she fell in love and lost, fighting over foreign soil, for France. 'The Auld Alliance' indeed. The count received both French and British awards and commendations for bravery and was honoured by the Russian Government after his untimely death, during the Second World War.

On 12 February 1942, the 'Ile de France' Squadron had another opportunity to fly in formation and create the Cross of Lorraine in the skies over the west coast of Scotland, for the benefit of General de Gaulle, General Valin and other senior French officers visiting the aerodrome at Ayr.

During March 1942, No. 340 under the command of Commandant de Scitivaux, moved south to the airfield at Merston, near Tangmere. Mouchotte was promoted to Captain. The squadron spent a short spell at Redhill before returning to Tangmere to take possession of brand-new Spitfires, Mark Vs.

Amongst the pilots then forming part of 340 Squadron were:

The CO, Commandant de Scitivaux
Captain Duperier
Captain Mouchotte
Captain de Labouchère
Captain Emile Fayolle
Bouquillard
Choron
Hauchemaille
Waillier
Bechoff

At the time, Mouchotte noted that Fayolle, Choron, de Labouchère and himself, were the four oldest Free French pilots.

From Tangmere on the 10 April 1942, under the command of Wing Commander Michael Robinson, 340 Squadron joined a massive group of British fighters over France. Attacked by a large number of Focke-Wulf Fw 190s, 340 Squadron joined in the battle. On their return to Tangmere the pilots received the news of the loss of Wing Commander Robinson, and Commandant de Scitivaux and Maurice Choron were missing. It was at this time that the 'Ile de France' Squadron was adopted by the City of Ottawa.

More daily sorties were flown from Tangmere, over France, resulting in pilot losses. Both Hauchemaille and Wallier failed to return to base. However, Captain Duperier, Emile Fayolle, Chauvin and Jean de Tedesco were each successful in shooting down Fw 190s.

In the latter part of May, 340 was joined by more young pilots, including André Moynet. The *Croix de Guerre* was awarded to Michel Boudier, Emile Fayolle, Coignard, Debec and de Tedesco.

News was received from France that Commandant de Scitivaux was alive and a prisoner.

Towards the end of July, General de Gaulle visited the 'Ile de France' at Tangmere.

A few days later, Commandant Duperier, who had taken over command of 340, after Commandant de Scitivaux had been shot down, was absent from the squadron's new base at Hornchurch in Essex and Mouchotte led the squadron on a sortie over France. They were attacked by over forty Fw 190s. They lost a number of Spitfires, several of which caught fire and crashed to the ground. One pilot managed to bale out, only to fall to his death when his parachute became engulfed in flames. Sous Lieutenant Lambert and Adjutant Debec were both missing after the day's sortie.

Chapter 3

Dieppe

Dawn came on 19 August 1942, as great preparations were made for the attack by the Canadian and French ground forces which were to be supported by a vast air armada of fighter aircraft. Endless sorties were flown throughout the day, giving air cover to the Army, landing on the beaches of Dieppe.

No. 340 'Ile de France' Squadron was operationally involved over the town of Dieppe, very early on, having taken off from Hornchurch aerodrome at about 04.30 hours, that morning. The aerial activity over the town was intense when the squadron, led by Commandant Duperier, arrived over Dieppe. Duperier, an escapee from France in 1940, had spent his early days in the RAF flying with No. 242 and No. 615 squadrons.

The Luftwaffe, very much in action and in large numbers, were attacking the British fighters whilst others harassed the ground forces. Lack of fuel forced the Hurricanes and Spitfires to retire from the battle zone in order to re-fuel at coastal aerodromes before returning to Dieppe.

Capitaine Emile Fayolle, twenty-five years of age and an old friend of Mouchotte from pre-war days, had recently been posted from No. 340 Squadron and had taken over command of No. 174 which was extremely active over the battle area. Fayolle was reported missing later that day, after his aircraft was last seen heading away from Dieppe, in the direction of the south coast of England. After the war, the French Authorities chose to name an avenue adjacent to the promenade at Dieppe, to the memory of Squadron Leader Emile Fayolle DFC.

With Mouchotte in command, 340 attacked the German fighters over Dieppe and Lieutenant Michel Boudier damaged an Fw 190. Capitaine de Labouchère shot down a Dornier Bomber and Sous Lieutenant Pierre Laureys was also successful in shooting down a Dornier. During another sortie Adjutant René Darbins, aged just twenty-one years and on his twenty-eighth operational flight, crashed into the sea, having been shot down.

During the withdrawal of air cover over Dieppe later in the day, several Free French pilots flying with other RAF squadrons were lost in action. French Pilot Officer Van Wymeerach, another twenty-one-year-old, crashed and was taken prisoner by the Germans. During the famous 'Great Escape' of RAF officers from Stalag III in 1944, Wymeerach managed to get away, only to be recaptured.

Pilot Officer Du Fretay, who had originally escaped from France in a light plane, was attacking gun emplacements at Dieppe, when his plane crashed and he was killed. Flight Sergeant Vilboux, born in Rennes and aged twenty-one, also an escapee from France in 1940, was attacked by an Fw 190 and crashed into the sea.

Later in the day, 340 Squadron completed its last sortie over the battle zone of Dieppe, returning to base at Hornchurch in Essex. From the enquiry that followed the operation, it was concluded that the British and Germans each lost approximately 100 aircraft which were shot down and destroyed. In reality, while the RAF did lose 100 aircraft, the Germans only lost 48.

The failure at Dieppe with the loss of so many Canadian and French-Canadian soldiers on the beachhead of this French port where so many were killed or taken prisoner during the battle, points quite clearly to the fact that Germans were aware an attack would be made on the French coast during the ideal tide and weather conditions which prevailed during the month of August. It must be said, in tribute to the Canadian troops, that those men had travelled vast distances, trained and waited in England for such an opportunity to fight for the freedom of France, only to make the supreme sacrifice at Dieppe. Their eventual retreat from the battle area resulted in quite a number of Canadians and French-Canadians refusing to cease fighting the enemy; they continued to attack the Germans in the streets, in and around Dieppe. Sadly, their patriotic resistance was soon overcome by the superior German armour.

In 1980, I had the privilege to visit their memorial, set on the promenade at Dieppe. My thoughts at the time, as I read the words on the monument, were to recall the stupidity of the planners and organisers who sent these troops to certain death or imprisonment in German stalags; the operation was doomed to failure before the invasion ships left English harbours. Perhaps I am prejudiced by family ties with Canada as my eldest brother was a Canadian and my feelings and sympathies must, therefore, be biased.

As the ground crews on the French Squadrons listened to the pilots describing the carnage they had witnessed as they flew at low level over Dieppe, they realised what a terrible waste of young Canadian lives had been exacted for such an operation.

The news that Squadron Leader Fayolle, had been reported missing as leader of No. 174 Squadron, reminded René Mouchotte that the RAF Fighter Command had originally offered him the post with 174 but he had declined to accept that command. Emile Fayolle had then accepted the opportunity. His reported loss left only de Labouchère and Mouchotte as the two survivors from the 'Old Gang' of Free French pilots of 1940.

Early in September 1942, Commandant Duperier became commanding officer of No. 340 Squadron, still based at Hornchurch. Mouchotte had been posted as squadron leader of No. 65 (East India) Squadron, stationed at Biggin Hill. He had been awarded the DFC to add to his *Croix de Guerre*. It was from Duperier that Mouchotte received the devastating news that an entire flight from 340 Squadron had been shot down over the Somme, attacked out of the sun by over forty Fw 190s. Several pilots were reported missing including Captain François de Labouchère, who was killed. French pilot Dubourgel did not return. With the previous loss of Emile Fayolle and now that of de Labouchère of the 'Old Gang', Mouchotte became the last surviving member of the little French group who had escaped to England together.

No. 65 Squadron was moved to the Scottish aerodrome at Drem where Mouchotte was able to visit his old friend, now wing commander, Loel Guinness, stationed at Turnhouse in Edinburgh. Later that month he was summoned south again and whilst in London he visited 340, still stationed at Biggin Hill.

At Biggin Hill he heard of the success rate of German aircraft shot down. André Moynet had recently shot down two Fw 190s. Flight Lieutenant Michel Boudier had added another two to his score. Commandant Duperier had increased his tally by two and Olivier Massart was credited with another German aircraft. Massart, a young man, had escaped from France in 1940, in the company of Captain François Labouchère. In 1944 Massart was promoted to command the 'Ile de France' Squadron in Europe.

On a visit to see General Valin, Mouchotte endeavoured to get himself posted back to the all Free French Squadron, without success.

Commandant Bernard Duperier was moved as CO of 340 in order to take up a more senior post in the establishment at Headquarters. Commandant Schloesing took over the command of No. 340 Squadron. In January 1943, the constant rumours about the formation of a second French Squadron became a reality and René Mouchotte was selected to be Commandant of No. 341 'Alsace', the second Free French Squadron in Scotland.

The nucleus of the new squadron was formed from Free French pilots already flying with other British Squadrons and they were joined by other compatriots coming in from units in North Africa. The original 'Alsace' Squadron had been formed in 1942 but was disbanded when operations ceased in North Africa. One of the Flight Commanders was Lieutenant Paul Ezanno, who later in his career, went on to command an RAF Typhoon Squadron.

It is interesting to point out at this stage, that in the course of my research, I was in contact by letter, with the former Group

Captain Desmond Scott, of New Zealand. In his letter of reply to me he stated that he had had a few Free French pilots in his No. 123 Typhoon Wing of the 2nd TAF, also some Free Belgian pilots. He specifically mentions one exceptional man on his wing: Paul Ezanno – 'the bravest man I ever met'. I found confirmation in the book by Desmond Scott, *Typhoon Pilot*, in which he recalls the bravery in action of Paul Ezanno. From his home in Christchurch, New Zealand, Scott states that Ezanno went on to become a general in the post-war French Air Force.

At the Fighter Command Headquarters in London, Mouchotte was asked to select his two flight commanders. To his amazement he discovered that pressure was being exerted by certain senior officers for him to accept two British flight commanders on an all French squadron. However, Mouchotte was adamant that the 'Alsace' flights should be led by Free Frenchmen and in spite of the pressure from higher sources, he nominated Flight Lieutenant Martel, (Martel being the 'nom de guerre' for the family name of Montet) and Flight Lieutenant Michel 'Bou-Bou' Boudier as the two Flight Commanders of the 'Alsace' Squadron. Martel was appointed CO of the 'Strasbourg' light and Boudier took command of the 'Mulhouse' Flight.

There was a great deal of difference between Mouchotte, a tall, dark, slim man with a unique sense of purpose and Christian Martel, a gentle giant of a man. They had done their military service together, in France in 1936. Martel had only just escaped from France with another friend of Mouchotte's, Dick Farman. Martel was a talented aerial tactician and an excellent fighter pilot.

Within a year he was to take command of No. 341 'Alsace' Squadron. Tragically his parents and family, involved with the Resistance movement in France, were betrayed to the Germans. He himself, very much involved in the resistance, was called upon to carry out secret operations which were not specifically to do with flying operations.

Admired by his fellow pilots, especially his friend Mouchotte and his British ground crew on 341, Commandant Christian Martel DFC, was killed in a flying accident on 31 August 1945, while France was enjoying her liberation. It was a great loss to the Free French wing. I am fortunate in having two photographs, taken early in 1944, on one of our south coast satellite airstrips, one of Martel, the other of Boudier.

After his visit to London Headquarters, Mouchotte returned to Drem in Scotland and from there moved on to Turnhouse, Edinburgh where the formation of No. 341 Free French Squadron was to begin. It was at this point that there seemed to be a hold-up in the supply of Spitfires, pilots and ground personnel. It was towards the middle of March 1943 before the Squadron began to take shape from an operational point of view, although it still had only half the normal strength of pilots.

Returning to Turnhouse after a brief visit to Flight Command in London, Mouchotte received the sad news of the death of French pilot de Mezillis, who had been killed in a flying accident over Scotland. This tragedy was twofold, as I was to learn when the story was retold to me in a letter I received in 1960, from the widow of one of the British ground crew, responsible for the Spitfire flown by de Mezillis, when it crashed near Turnhouse in March 1943.

Mrs Helen Archibald told me in her letter that her late husband, Robert (Archie) Archibald, a Scot from Edinburgh and an armourer on 341 Squadron, had been very friendly with his pilot, Jacques de Mezillis, who had had his arm amputated as a result of being on operations in Libya earlier in the war and, therefore, flew his aircraft with an artificial arm.

In order to fly the aircraft, de Mezillis was required to have his artificial arm secured to the control column of the Spitfire. When a fault developed in the wings of the aircraft and he was forced to crash land over Scotland, he had died with his Spitfire. He had been unable to bale out as the plane crashed to the ground at full speed. Jacques de Mezillis was buried with full military honours at Corstorphine Cemetery in Edinburgh.

Robert Archibald died in 1979, after a long illness. He never really overcame the loss of his friend and pilot who died in 1943.

In 1986 I had the opportunity of meeting Helen Archibald, a delightful lady and her daughter and grandchildren, in their home in the outskirts of Edinburgh. Helen Archibald gave me her encouragement and permission to include this personal story concerning her husband, whom she met during 341 Squadron's stay at Turnhouse. It is in his memory that I included this account and to give his grandchildren the opportunity of reading about their grandfather; in armourers' jargon – 'a plumber to the end.'

On 17 March 1943, No. 341 'Alsace' Squadron moved from Turnhouse to Biggin Hill in the south of England, replacing No. 340 'Ile de France'. Flying operations began on 18 March.

Amongst the compliment of trained pilots were some veterans from 340 – Martel and Farman who escaped together from

France the year before. Henri Lafont from 341 had recently returned from Libya, a brave and distinguished pilot and close friend of Mouchotte. Lieutenant Michel Boudier, Lieutenant Bougen and other veterans including Raoul Duval, Chevalier and Bruno Bourges. The Station Commander at Biggin Hill was Group Captain Malan with Wing Commander Alan Deere, both fighter aces from the Battle of Britain. Under their command were: de Bordes, Roos, Mathey, Savary, Bourges, Gallet, Pabiot, Marquis, Bougen, Farman, Chevalier, Clostermann, Girardon, Beraud, Laurent, Mailfert, Duval, Lafont, Buiron, Legui, Borne, Commailles, Artaud, Remlinger, Martel.

Whilst 340 was based at Biggin Hill it had a great deal of success and it was inevitable that the squadron pilots needed to be rested from flying operations, not only from physical but mental fatigue. This rest and peace was available at Turnhouse which was to be the next move.

It transpired that during their spell at Biggin Hill, the squadron lost more pilots than the German aircraft they shot down. The CO, Commandant Schloesing, was lost in these operations, shot down over Le Touquet, although news reached base that he was safe in Switzerland.

When 340 'Ile de France' returned to Turnhouse in Scotland, the newsmen again moved in for their stories. As 340 was the first Free French Squadron to be formed at Turnhouse in November 1941, the reporters were eager to talk to the pilots and collect copy of their exploits in the south, whilst at Biggin Hill and Hornchurch.

On Saturday, 3 April 1943, *The Scotsman* newspaper featured a front page, banner headline and a photograph of two senior Free French pilots displaying the squadron flag on which a *Croix de Guerre* medal had been pinned. The flag was a gift to the squadron by a French Association in Great Britain and the collective award of the *Croix de Guerre* with the *fourragère* given to all members of the squadron, was presented to 340 at Hornchurch, by General Charles de Gaulle, for the excellent air cover given to the ground forces during the Dieppe battle.

The Scotsman ran another headline: 'Fighting French Airmen – Ile de France Squadron's links with Scotland.' The Air Correspondent of the paper had the pleasure of being welcomed to Turnhouse aerodrome by the squadron commandant, the rank that corresponds to a squadron leader in the RAF. This particular commandant, whose home was in Savoy, had taken part in seventy-six sweeps over France. Whilst in the south, operating from Biggin Hill and Hornchurch, 340 had completed over 200 sorties.

The commandant described his pilots as being first class, many having escaped from France although the stories of how they reached English shores could not be told. Many had experience with *L'Armée de l'Air* in pre-war France. The ground crews were represented as being more cosmopolitan consisting of Frenchmen, Englishmen and innumerable Scots!

Mention was made in the article of one lieutenant pilot who was on the staff of a well-known French newspaper and of the adjutant of 340, being married to a Scottish lady and having a French mother and a father from Lancashire. When the correspondent commented to the adjutant that this was a re-birth of the 'Auld Alliance' he just nodded and smiled.

It was while 340 was stationed at Biggin Hill that the squadron took its toll of the German planes shot down and numerous pilots were lost in air sweeps over France. Of these, Lieutenant Lambert, who was shot down over his own country, managed to bale out and land safely. He was able to make his way to his home in France, where he stayed for some time, before escaping back to England.

Another remarkable adventure was that of a veteran from the first 'Alsace' Squadron, Lieutenant Raoul Duval, who after being shot down, baled out and made a successful landing in France. During his time there, he married his fiancée and re-escaped to England with his new bride.

There are many exciting tales of escape, however, not all the pilots were successful in their attempts, due primarily, to betrayal to the Gestapo, often involving close friends and sometimes relatives who took the 'thirty pieces of silver.' Some of the more heroic stories uncovered in my many years of research cannot be related as I have no wish to re-open unhappy memories for the pilots' families, still living in France.

One particular episode concerned a well-known, successful French fighter pilot who made his original escape the long way round, so to speak. Arriving in England he joined the squadron and was shot down on two separate occasions but in each case was able to re-escape after a short imprisonment by the Germans. Tragically, on another sweep over France, later in the year, he was again forced to bale out from his aircraft which crashed in his own country. Although badly injured he landed safely and was in hiding but was subsequently caught and executed by the Germans. He had been betrayed by another Frenchman.

Installed at Biggin Hill in the middle of March 1943, No. 341 (Alsace) Squadron, soon began sweeps over France, in very strict battle formations, taking on the Fw 190s and Bf 109s. Some twenty-four aircraft operated from Biggin Hill, commanded by Commandant Mouchotte on these sorties, but it was rare for the German Luftwaffe to accept battle unless they were sure of numerical superiority, tactics and altitude.

It was on one of these sweeps over France by 341, that French pilot Raoul Duval was shot down in flames over Le Havre, the area in which he lived in peacetime. Pilot Beraud was lost on the same operation. He was seen to leave the battle area, heading south, with engine failure. These two men were the first to be lost since 341 left Turnhouse.

During operations from Biggin Hill on 14 May 1943, Flight Commander Christian Martel of 341, shot down an Fw 190 over Courtrai in Belgium, bringing the total number of enemy aircraft shot down by British aircraft operating from Biggin Hill since the war began to 997.

The following day, 15 May 1943, during further sweeps over France, both 341 and 611 squadrons operating from Biggin Hill, suddenly encountered several *staffeln* of German fighters, encircling the outskirts of Le Havre. Commandant René Mouchotte leading 341 Squadron, saw a German Fw 190 slide across his aircraft and into the range of his guns. He reacted instantly and flames ran along the fuselage of the Focke-Wulf, which immediately exploded and disintegrated in the air.

On his return to base, Mouchotte reported to operations and discovered that Squadron Leader Charles of 611 Squadron had also shot down two German aircraft. It was therefore concluded that Mouchotte had dispatched the 'Thousandth' German aircraft shot down from Biggin Hill.

Later the same month, on another successful sweep over Caen, Mouchotte shot down a Bf 109. Returning to base, he heard that both Boudier and Bougen had shot one down. On the same mission, a young Free French pilot, Sergeant Bourges, failed to return but was seen to bale out of his aircraft.

On several occasions during this period of 1943, Mouchotte commanded the Biggin Hill Wing, comprising of at least thirty-six aircraft. On these operations, the wing was used in the capacity of giving air cover to the American Flying Fortresses, bombing targets on and around airfields of the Luftwaffe in France, Belgium and Holland. This type of operation continued for several weeks, with Mouchotte in charge of the four squadrons.

It is interesting to note that amongst the Free French pilots of 341 'Alsace' Squadron, who were in the thick of any air battle with the Germans, René Mouchotte found time to select and give encouragement to one Sergeant Pierre Clostermann – one of his 'young men', as Mouchotte described his pilots. In 1943 he wrote that: 'Sergeant Clostermann should go far'. Mouchotte's foresight was correct in so much that during 1944-1945, Clostermann became the commander of a British Typhoon squadron and, when the war came to an end, entered politics.

At the end of July 1943, the wing from Biggin Hill, comprising No. 485 'New Zealand' and No. 341 'Alsace', led by Commandant Mouchotte; they were on a sweep over Lisieux, when some sixty German aircraft appeared out of the sun. The Spitfires and Fw 190s at altitudes of over 20,000 feet, engaged in a dogfight. After a short time, five German planes were shot down by the pilots of 341, and the New Zealanders of 485 accounted for another four. No losses were sustained by either squadron on this occasion.

Later that day, Commandant Mouchotte received a telegram at Biggin Hill, addressed to the wing, from Prime Minister Winston Churchill, in which he congratulated them with the words, 'Nine for nought is an excellent result'.

It is understandable that with the intensity of the daily sweeps over France and the Low Countries, the strain of continuous operations at high altitudes had an extremely adverse effect on the nerves of the pilots and their physical well-being was stretched to breaking point. Commandant René Mouchotte, as CO of 341 'Alsace' and sometimes leader of the whole of the Biggin Hill Wing, was frequently called upon to lead two or three squadrons, several times a week, on operations ever occupied territory. By August 1943, he had reached the record figure of some 150 daily sweeps since his arrival as CO at Biggin Hill and he had been operationally active for two years without a rest from flying.

On one of the August sweeps over France, one of 341's flight commanders, Lieutenant Christian Martel, attacked and shot down an Fw 190, only to discover later that the pilot was Major Graf von Richthofen, commander of the famous German Richthofen squadron and fighter ace of the Luftwaffe. He crashed in flames on his own German airfield.

During this month the intensity of the sweeps was stepped up with disastrous results for our fighter squadrons. By operating further into Europe, our planes and pilots were more at risk, so far from home, than were the German pilots who were flying from local airfields in their own backyard.

On 27 August 1943, No. 341 'Alsace' with No. 485 'New Zealand' Squadron, under the command of Commandant René Mouchotte as leader of the wing, took off from Biggin Hill, to escort a large formation of American Flying Fortresses, on an operation to bomb St Omer in France. Shortly after arriving over the area, approximately 200 Fw 190s attacked the New Zealand and French Squadrons and very quickly the Spitfires were swamped by the German aircraft on a ratio of some twenty to one.

Flying as number two wingman on 341, to Commandant Mouchotte on this sortie, was Sergeant Pierre Clostermann. A dog-fight developed and he lost contact with his leader and was never seen again. Sous Lieutenant Laurent, who was also attacked, saw Sergeant Chef Magrot shot down by an Fw 190.

When the remnants of both 341 and 485 squadrons eventually returned to base, they found the station commander Group Captain 'Sailor' Malan, Wing Commander Alan Deere (New Zealand) and Wing Commander Johnnie Checketts (New Zealand), waiting for news of the wing. Both squadrons had first landed at Manston before returning to Biggin Hill.

After waiting anxiously for some time after the landing of the last Spitfire, it became unhappily, quite evident to all, Free French pilots and ground crews alike, that the former flight commander of 340 'Ile de France', then CO of 341 'Alsace' Squadron, Commandant René Mouchotte, *Croix de Guerre*, DFC, had been lost over the battle area of St Omer in France.

This then, could have been the sad end of the story concerning René Mouchotte, hero of France, a great loss to both the French and the RAF. However, after the war had ended, many French pilots and dignitaries paid homage to Mouchotte in written articles and references in books published in France.

Commandant (now Colonel) Bernard Duperier, former CO of 340 Squadron, who took over the command of 341 'Alsace', following Mouchotte's death, General Valin the former Chief of Staff of the Free French Air Forces, former Commandant Pierre Clostermann and many other former Allied pilots, all paid tribute to this Frenchman's (a Parisian) courage, leadership and supreme sacrifice for France and for freedom.

Mouchotte the leader was dead. But his memory was immortalised when an old family friend André Dezarrois asked Mouchotte's mother, soon after the war ended, if he could publish her son's diaries under the title in France of *Les Carnets de René Mouchotte*, which, as I have already stated, have since been published in English. Some years after the publication of the diaries, I began my own research into the life of René Mouchotte, the former CO of the French squadrons on which I served as a member of the ground crew. This acted as a catalyst for me to complete this book.

My quest took me to virtually every aerodrome that Commandant Mouchotte and the Free French pilots had been stationed at during the last war. Time, for me, was of the essence, however, and I had not envisaged how difficult and lengthy my task would prove to be.

I had read the diaries and was fortunate enough to have had correspondence with two former Free French pilots of 341 Squadron, namely Henri Lafont, one of the original escapees from Oran with Mouchotte and André Moynet. I had the additional advantage of being able to contact the former CO of No. 145 French Wing – Group Captain Loel Guinness. When I asked him if he would be prepared to write the foreword to my book, he readily agreed.

My travels took me far and wide from Turnhouse, Drem and Ayr in Scotland, throughout England to Biggin Hill, Hornchurch, Manston, Martlesham, Rochford, Kenley, Tangmere, Merston, Funtingdon, Church Norton and Chichester. Over the Channel to Normandy, Sommervieu, Bernay, Abbeville, Lille, through to Wevelgem near Courtrai and Deurne near Antwerp in Belgium. On to Schjindel in Holland, Lingen in Germany until I reached Fassberg near Hanover where the Free French Squadrons were disbanded in November 1945.

I have met and talked with a number of former pilots and ground crews over the years, and each had a story to relate. In the latter pages of this book, I have included some of the anecdotes relative to life on the Free French squadrons during the last war.

On 27 August 1943, when Mouchotte was lost over St Omer, it was presumed that he had been shot down and had crashed into the sea. This was basically true; his plane had indeed gone into the sea. However, some seven days later, a pilot's body was washed up on the beach and found opposite the Belle Vue Hotel at Westende-Plage, Middelkerke in Belgium. The date was 3 September 1943.

In 1980 I travelled to Paris and visited the cemetery at Père-Lachaise, where in October 1949, the body of the late René Mouchotte was lain to rest in the family vault, having been returned from the soil of Belgium. To see René Mouchotte's photograph inside the vault was a very moving experience.

Some three years later, I was in Belgium to continue my research and, one morning, I went to the Hotel Belle Vue, Westende-Plage at Middelkerke. The sandy beach directly outside the hotel was where a pilot's body had been washed up on the morning of 3 September 1943.

Following on from an introduction by the manager of the hotel, I met a gentleman who lives in Middelkerke, Carlo Van Troostenberghe a former librarian in the town. He had spent some of the war years in a German labour camp.

Carlo had no love for the Germans. In our conversation I discovered that he too, had researched the story of René Mouchotte and like me, had begun by visiting the grave at Père Lachaise in Paris.

Carlo and his son Ronny had an interest in a local magazine, produced on a subscription basis for the local area. A copy, printed in Flemish, was given to me. It contained the Mouchotte story. Carlo generously outlined the strange facts relating to the pilot's body which was found on the beach and subsequently buried in the Belgian town of Middelkerke, by members of the German garrison.

The true identity of the pilot said to have been found on the beach outside the Belle Vue Hotel is given in some detail in the *Mouchotte Diaries*. Standing on the spot where the Belgian civilians originally found the body, gave credence and understanding as to why this pilot died so mysteriously. Amazingly it took six years after Mouchotte had been reported missing, to discover that the pilot on the beach was indeed the late René Mouchotte, former Commander of 341 'Alsace' Squadron. [This fascinating story is told in Dilip Sarkar and Jan Leeming's aforementioned book.]

In the little town of Middelkerke, I spoke to the town clerk who was pleased to show me the monument in the foyer of the town hall, still surrounded with flowers, to the memory of René Mouchotte. Moreover, such was the admiration of the townspeople, that an Avenue in Middelkerke is named R. Mouchottelaan.

On the 28 August 1943, Commandant Bernard Duperier took over command of 341 'Alsace' Squadron. It was his difficult and painful task to prepare the previous day's combat report and to describe how the loss of the former CO of the squadron affected the young pilots of this Free French Unit.

At this time 340 Squadron was at Drem and was moved to Ayr in August 1943, before returning once again to Drem. In November it moved to Perranporth and early in 1944, to Merston adjacent to Tangmere in West Sussex.

During the early months of 1944 an all Free French wing, No. 145, had been integrated into the 2nd Tactical Air Force, containing 340 Squadron under the command of Commandant Fournier, *Croix de Guerre*, 341 Squadron under the command of Commandant Christian Martel and 329 Free French Squadron under the command of Commandant Fleurquin, who had arrived with that squadron at the port of Greenock on the 5 January 1944, after service in North Africa.

The majority of 329's pilots consisted of:

Captain Ozanne
Lieutenants Avon, Marchelidon, Billoin, Souviat, Caropino, Tanguy, Carpentier, Trulla
Sous Lieutenant Crozet
Adjutant Chef Cheminade
Sergeant Chefs Alligier, Figirere, Mazo, Bourachav, Kerquelen, Richard, Debrot, Lombaert, Saigne
Sergeants Robardey and Buham
The intelligence officer for the squadron was Captain P. Rouxel

From 12 January 1944 the pilots were posted to various officer training units for refresher courses before 329 Squadron joined 145 Wing at Perranporth, where a further group of new French pilots arrived from No. 57 Officer Training Unit, bringing the squadron establishment up to thirty-one pilots.

This latest group comprised of:

Sous Lieutenant Kulling
Aspirant Roger
Sous chefs Camus, Tavernier, Marchal, Rose
Lieutenant Muzard

The entire 145 Wing was moved from Perranporth to Merston, a satellite airfield. It was there that on 18 April 1944, a new pilot, Sous Lieutenant De Segonzac from No. 611 Squadron joined No. 329.

Later that same month, on 26 April 1944, the wing suffered a day of tragedy. The squadrons were ordered to escort a number of Martin B-26 Marauder bombers, en route to attack a railway junction at Mons. The squadrons (Nos. 329 and 340) took off but before leaving the English coastline, Sergeant Chef Alligier collided in cloud formation with Wing Commander Marples who was leading the wing. Wing Commander Marples crashed and was killed but Sergeant Chef Alligier was fortunate to make a forced landing at Shoreham.

On another sortie the same day, Adjutant Chef Cheminade, a pilot of considerable experience, having flown as a fighter pilot for over ten years, before joining 329 in February 1943 and extremely popular and well liked amongst his fellow pilots, was seen to crash into the sea a few miles south of St Catherine's Point. Cheminade was not seen to get out of his aircraft and was presumed killed. It was a sad loss to the squadron so early on in operations, to lose their wing commander in such a horrendous accident followed by the death of the other experienced pilot.

By 30 April 1944, the wing was fortunate to have as replacement Wing Commander 'Bill' Crawford Compton. He was to undertake a considerable period of operations with the Free French wing, right through to the Normandy landings and into Europe.

Early in May 1944, the French wing, led by Wing Commander Compton, took off from Manston and flew to Bradwell Bay, where they escorted a group of B-25 Mitchell bombers, heading towards Belgium to attack the railway station at Namur. Shortly after leaving the target area, Commandant Fleurquin, leading 329 Squadron, collided with another aircraft between Namur and Mons. The other plane, flown by Sous Lieutenant Reeve of 340, was seen to go down with half his starboard wing missing.

Commandant Fleurquin, escorted by Commandant Martel who was leading 341, managed with great difficulty, to bring his aircraft to the edge of the English coast, where he baled out near the village of Denton in Kent and was quite safe.

Such then is the story of René Mouchotte and 341 Squadron. What follows is the part played in this story by me, a boy from Islington.

Chapter 4

A Boy from Islington

I was born at 162 Barnsbury Road, Islington, N1. The youngest son of Alf and Florence Chapman, I arrived on 26 April 1924. I had three elder brothers and one sister who over my early years took it in turn to bully, patronize and ignore me. Both my parents were born in Islington. My father was born in 1881 at the top end of the Caledonian Road, N7 whilst my mother, born in 1885, had a house in Islington Green as her birthplace. By a strange chain of events both my parents were taken as young children to live in Southend-on-Sea, Essex, by their respective families. When my mother and father married, it was in Southend-on-Sea, but they returned with their, then, three children, to live in Islington. My father's occupation was coachman, whilst my mother was a housewife, cleaner, char lady and cook etc.

My earliest recollections are of being taken in an old pram around the streets by my brother Ernie and his pals, and being tipped out of the pram in Cloudesley Road, N1 as the gang tried to negotiate a kerbstone. Ernie was nine years older than me and did not take kindly to being a nurse-maid to me when he really wanted to be playing cricket or climbing trees with his friends.

My eldest brother Alex was some twenty-two years older than me, and I have a vague memory of him standing on the kitchen table and making me jump into his arms as he stood further and further away from the table. Fortunately for me, he never failed to catch me. I was about three years old although the event is still clear in my mind. Sadly, for me, he left home and emigrated to Canada in 1927, after one of the many arguments he had with my father. I never saw him again and I felt a great loss when he died in Canada in the 1970s.

My first school was at Barnsbury Park School at the top end of Thornhill Road, (at the time of writing an all-girls' school). The year was 1929, the year famous for the Wall Street Crash. Ernie my brother, attended the same school but left at fifteen, a year after I had joined the school.

I never really liked school, mostly because I suffered very badly from a nervous disability and continuously attended the outpatients' department of the children's section of the University College Hospital, near Euston Station. One of the effects of my nervous disorder was that I suffered extremely badly from stammering and stuttering, which unfortunately for me prevailed for many years until I was about fifteen years of age and to a more or lesser degree, up until the present day.

This disastrous impediment was to play havoc with my early school years, and I became singled out at school by the school bully and his cronies at whichever school I attended later on. Although of no help to me I was not alone with this speech sediment as there were several other boys and girls in my class who also suffered from the same problem. With hindsight, I can only imagine that a great many children born in the 1920s, who suffered the terrible plight of stammering, were the aftereffects of having fathers who had served in the First World War and returned home after the war suffering from the effects of being shell-shocked.

I had a teacher called Miss Martingale, who realized my terrible predicament and a headmistress, Mrs Baker, who took pity on our little group of stutterers and each Friday, when school had ended for the week, would invite two of us to have tea with her in her study. She was very kind to me in my agony when called upon to speak. On each occasion I was invited to tea, I enjoyed the tea but hated the cake, which was always seed cake. I moved up to the all-boys' part of the school and the situation became more acute, being the butt of any joke, both from the bullies and teachers alike. When I was nine years of age, the authorities closed Barnsbury Park School and we were all transferred to Thornhill Road School for Boys, where the situation went from bad to worse.

On one occasion a teacher took it upon himself to hold me out of the window of our first floor classroom because I found it impossible to answer his question. My mother, in her despair at my unwillingness to go to school the following day, related the window incident to my father, who being a very strong, aggressive and short-tempered man, took time off from work, marched me to school, and the said teacher found himself confronted with my father, who grabbed the teacher and held him out or the same window. A great commotion arose as the teacher, a little white around the gills, was again threatened with more of the same if he laid his hands on me again.

Fortunately for me, my grandmother found another school, St Thomas' Boys' School in Everilda Street, Islington, where

I received a more sympathetic education, and which indeed was the beginning of my eventual cure to my nervous stammering.

Some months after I had changed schools, my stammering seemed to ease slightly, and I joined with a little gang of kids who lived in Barnsbury Road. On Thursdays in the hall in Dowrey Street, the local vicar put on a magic lantern show to be followed by indoor games, which included table tennis, boxing, etc. Mainly because there was nothing else to do, a lot of the boys, including me would troop in for the lantern show, just to get the chance to use the various forms of sports equipment. It was here that I believe Christianity entered my life. Up until I started going every Thursday to the hall, religion never featured in my life.

Table tennis became my interest, and I became extremely good, bearing in mind the local opposition. Although I had changed schools, most of the boys I played with still went mostly to Thornhill Road School and amongst the boys who lived close to me, was one by the name of Georgie Wood, whose family seemed to be involved in amateur boxing.

It had been a difficult time because on many occasions a boy called Wood, who was slightly older than me, enjoyed the opportunity of bullying boys younger and smaller than himself. Several times, with his gang of pals, he would attack me when I was alone, and I would go home with all sorts of cuts and bruises. My mother patched me up but never mentioned the incident to my father, until one evening when I returned home, looking very much the worse for wear. Mother's reaction was to ask who had hit me and to tell me that I had to stand and fight this boy Wood and beat him or my father would give me a good hiding. While I didn't fancy either alternative, I knew I had to stand up for myself or get a walloping from my dad.

I continued to go to the Thursday evening lantern show at the hall in Dowrey Street, and on one occasion I was playing table tennis, when Wood, with two of his pals appeared in the hall and started to pick on one boy, much younger than himself. Remembering the threat of my dad's potential punishment, I took on the role of defending the younger boy. Whereupon, Wood, threatened to beat me up. The vicar, hearing the commotion, suggested that both Wood and I should settle the argument in the boxing ring, which was situated in the basement of the hall. Very quickly, a ring was put together and boxing gloves brought out but although I waited for my opponent to appear, Wood stayed upstairs in the main hall. Although Wood was making threats of what he was going to do to me, he still didn't appear, and I went up to the main hall twice before he agreed to enter the boxing ring. Finally, with several other boys and a lot of noise, he entered the ring. With the vicar acting as referee the contest began.

The first round was fairly even but although he was taller and bigger than me, I found that I could hit him quite easily. With his band of supporters encouraging him on, Wood began the second round a little apprehensively. He suddenly realized that I was as good, if not better than him and I was lighter and very quick on my feet. Halfway through the round, Wood came at me, head down, obviously determined not to lose face with his pole and to knock my head off. It was now I realized I had hurt his pride more than anything as he came head-on.

I sidestepped his rush and brought up in almighty undercut, which fortunately for me, connected with his mouth. Blood spurted all over me and the vicar quickly stepped in and stopped the fight. When I looked at Wood I found he had collapsed on the floor and was minus a few teeth. His pals carried him away, and I had to admit that I felt elated.

My own injuries were a slightly bruised mouth and on taking off the glove on my right hand, I discovered that I had hit Wood so hard that the thumb of the glove had split open, and Wood's teeth had cut my thumb. The vicar made us shake hands in true sporting fashion and Wood left the hall with about half of his original band of supporters, the others had obviously switched sides. Later on, I heard rumours from some of the boys, that Wood had made threats as to what his elder brother would do to me the following day, but surprisingly enough, nothing happened. Returning home, my mother was shocked by the blood on my shirt and my slight injuries, but I recall my father's eyes twinkled when I went into great detail, explaining to him how I beat the bully, Wood. Virtually from that time onwards my life changed, and I joined a boxing club, which was run by the Catholic priest, who lived on the corner of Everilda Street and Matilda Street, N1.

The only snag was, that to belong to the club, boys had to attend Sunday morning Mass. My parents were not keen on this stipulation, but eventually my father agreed I could join the boxing club. It was in the early days at the club that a team of boxers came to the club from a boxing club on Chapel Street, Islington, and challenged us to series of bouts at different age groups. I remember, that amongst the boys from the Chapel

Street Club, was an extremely good boxer, called Terry Govier, who went on to become British, Commonwealth, European and World flyweight champion after the Second World War, under the name of Terry Allen.

Continuing with my schooling at St Thomas', I was put into class where most of the other boys lived in streets nearby, although many lived in the Caledonia Road (The Caley). Our teacher was Mr Robinson, whose mother was headmistress of the infants at St Thomas'.

The majority of the boys I went to school with were from large families. It was quite normal to find that as many as six or eight brothers and sisters were at the school in different classes. In one family there were twenty, with at least nine children of varying ages, attending school.

Very few boys ever had new clothes. Poverty surrounded the area. In my class more than half the boys had free school dinners and class distinction was rearing its head, even then. The boys who paid four pence, old money, received a blue ticket, whilst the free dinner boys, as they were called, got the larger green ticket and their names were called out and put in register. I was fortunate and one of the lucky ones to go home to dinner, whilst 'free dinner boys' trouped up to Victoria Street School for their dinner.

I liked our teacher, Mr Robinson, he was about twenty-four years of age when I first joined his class and knowing my previous school history, he encouraged me. He would give me odd jobs to do which helped my confidence to do well in whatever lesson came along.

On one occasion, we had to write a story about any subject we liked. I recall doing an essay on the lifeboatmen. Surprisingly enough, it received top marks of all the essays from the class and sometime later, without my knowledge, it was entered in a content with entries from all the schools within the London County Council. It won first prize. On reflection, it was my first literary article.

As time went on, I moved up to the next class with Mr Roe, (Kipper, friendly nickname), the headmaster as our teacher. He was a marvellous man, strict but fair. He had been in the navy in the First World War, and still suffered from a slight shell shock, which took the form of a twitching in his neck. He was a man I came to respect. Often, when he gave us a lesson which was boring, one of the boys, being aware of Kipper's stories of the First World War and his personal experiences, would deliberately, at the beginning of the lesson, ask a question about the First World War, whereupon, for perhaps the whole of the lesson, he would have an audience of boys hanging on in his every word, as he related incidents that had happened to him during the war, which sometimes went on until the end of school time.

Because there had been another elder boy at the school with the same surname as me, who for some odd reason had the nickname of 'Whiggie' it followed that when he left school, this nickname transferred itself to be. From that time, I became Whiggie Chapman and, as I got to know the boys at school a lot better, I would leave my friends in Barnsbury Road and gradually it became a habit to return to the area of the Caley to play with my schoolmates, after school and during weekends and school holidays.

One boy I was friendly with was called Marjoram who lived on Muriel Street and one day he asked me home for tea. He was a friendly boy but very poor. When we got to his house the front door key was on the usual long piece of string which he pulled through the letter box and opened the door. The picture I saw has never left me. As I have said, most of the kids I went to school with were poor, so it was just the way it was, and nobody worried whether the kids were setting enough to eat, nobody cared.

As we walked along the passage into the back room, I saw an old pine table, worn with years of wear. On it, a beer bottle with a candle stuck in the neck, which Marjoram lit. A chunk of bread, an old saucer which held a slab of yellow margarine, and a jampot containing a very violent red jam with a couple of knives and several mugs, some minus handle, were all that I could see. Apart from few chairs, the room was bare of anything resembling furniture or curtains.

Marjoram boiled a kettle on a black gas stove covered in assorted lavers of fat, which ran and congealed as the heat melted the grease. We had bread and jam and talked. I liked Marjoram. He had nothing, yet he offered me tea at his house and his friendship. The houses in Muriel Street have all now disappeared and new houses have been built but I will always remember the really poor boy who had nothing and was not only hungry for food but for a friend to take home for tea. I have never forgotten him.

Every few months our school was paid a visit by the 'Nit Nurse', which meant lining up and waiting your turn to have metal comb immersed in disinfectant drawn several times through your hair, looking for the lice that appeared in some boys' hair and inspecting clothing for members of the 'Red Coat Brigade' (bedbugs). On one occasion one boy was found to have a vest, shirt and three sweaters, all sewn together. In some families, where there were several brothers, it was not unusual for two out of three brothers only to attend school because there was only enough clothing for two. Footwear was invariably boots, often many sizes too large.

In the Caledonian Road stood the local baths, one section for swimming, the other for hot baths, where soap and clean towels were supplied. It cost two pence, old money, to enter. As part of the school curricula, Wednesday afternoons, after the first lesson, were devoted to swimming instruction at the baths. The whole class would line up waiting for the teacher to march us from school to the baths. Those who had costumes and towels were usually leading the way whilst the rest had something like an old sheet under their arm. For boys who could swim, it was an excellent opportunity to exercise their skill, but those, including me, who couldn't swim, took a long time to undress, tied knots in our shoe or boot laces to waste time before the teacher came along to make us enter the water.

To teach non-swimmers, the teacher would use a long pole with a leather loop attached to one end, which the boy would loop over his head and, supported around the middle of his body, would attempt a few strokes. Unfortunately, the boy would often move out of his depth and slip out of the leather sling, resulting in ducking for the boy and desperate attempts by the teacher and other swimmers to save him from sinking further to the bottom of the pool. Afterwards there would be a run to get changed and try to be first at the cake shop at the bottom of Richmond Road, opposite the Bertolle photographers shop. They always seemed to have an endless pile of stale cakes, which the boys with a halfpenny would buy and share out with the less fortunate.

With St Thomas's being a Church of England school, religion was very much to the fore and as the church was opposite the school, it became normal for the boys to proceed out of the school gates, across Everilda Street into the church. The priest, at this time, was the Reverend Flynn, who lived at the vicarage at the top end of Richmond Road, very near to Barnsbury Gardens. I don't believe many of us were converted to Christianity, but for me, Flynn had spent a great deal of his life in various parts of Africa as a missionary, and I quickly became interested in his stories of his life with the Africans. To add colour to his tales, he always had a supply of spears, axes, and other weapons, used by the different tribes, which he allowed us to handle. Later on in my life, this church, which is sadly no more, became a symbol to me during the early years of the Second World War.

During the summer evenings the tennis courts in Dowrey Street, at the top end of Richmond Road, were used a great deal and it was not long before I got the job of ball-boy, retrieving the tennis balls which went over the netting into the street outside. This earned me a few pennies each evening, plus the deposit money which I received on returning the empty Tizer bottles to the sweet shop in Cloudesley Road, Islington.

As Dowrey Street did not have any houses in the street, it became a meeting place for any of us boys during school holidays. On some occasions, us boys would go into Chapel Street and in single file, would trail our hands along the fronts of the greengrocer's stalls and if you were lucky, an orange or apple would stick to your fingers. Sometimes, as a bonus, a banana would be taken off the stall. If you were unlucky, it would be a clip round the ear from the nearest stallholder with the threat to knock 'Your bloody 'ead off'.

When we were completely unsuccessful, a few spuds would be found in the gutter and taken back to Dowrey Street. A baked bean tin with a lump of string tied at the top, held the potato and from the newsagents we would pinch all the loose papers outside. A fire would then be lit and us boys would take it in turns to hold the tin over the blazing newspapers. The spuds never really cooked but became scorched, blackened and generally burnt, and indeed so did we, and we all took it in turns to bite a chunk out of it and went home with singed hair and eyebrows, and covered in soot.

Sunday mornings were always interesting as the first noise that broke the silence was the milkman, who made his presence known in the streets by bawling out 'Milko'. To those who wanted milk, the milkman's cries always started an onslaught of kids running down the thread-bare steps of the tenements, grasping a chipped or broken jug in one hand and, clutched in his other grubby hand, the pennies to pay for the milk, which was ladled out by the milkman from his three-wheeled cart, containing large metal jugs. He had a simple rule of thumb – no credit, no jug or container meant no milk. The milkman moved slowly from house to house along Barnsbury Road. The next roaring sound came from the Boy Scouts' band, the trumpeters blowing their brains out, trying to keep in tune, whilst the lanky kid at the rear of the band was dead set on smashing in the sides of the big drum. The rest of the scouts of varying sizes, were either banging symbols or smashing side-drums, fighting to keep in step with the scout leader who was dressed in shorts that were either too short, with a waistband up under his armpits, or voluminous to the point that with a good gust of wind, he would have become airborne. Eventually, at the band passed into Thornhill Road, the crashing and banging would slowly fade in the distance. Peace would return for about fifteen minutes only to be broken again by a second onslaught from the Boys' Brigade, exercising their lungs and beating their drums, determined to outdo the scouts' band, which had just moved on.

Both these bands would form up on comer by Pulteney Street and Barnsbury Road and were well into their second wind by the time they reached the 'Eclipse' public house, next door to 162 Barnsbury Road, where I lived. A lull is marching activity would then be followed by the bells of Trinity Church, Cloudesley Road, joined later on by the bells from St Thomas's, Hemingford Road. By this time, one could assume that anyone not awake or moving around was dead.

As I grew older, I began to move into other streets which run off from the Caley, Lyon Street, Gifford Street, Lofting Road, Bingfield Street, Stanford Street, etc. This was mainly because some of the boys I was at school with lived in the tenements which existed there and I was reasonably safe from getting beaten up by some of the other kids who went to Gifford Street School and Blundell Street School.

During the holiday periods from school a gang of boys from the Caley, including me, would go round the various streets following the horse carts. The object was to collect the horse-shit as it became available and flog it to the occupants of the posh houses in the top end of Barnsbury Park, a road running off Thornhill Road. Whatever money we got we would share between us. Or alternatively, we would break up wooden boxes and sell the wood to the old ladies to light their fires. This was one certain way of getting enough money to visit the 'Co-Bo', a flea pit of a cinema, situated on the corner of Copenhagen Street and Caledonian Road.

The Saturday morning picture show would always bring in a crowd of kids from all directions and a queue would form from about 08.00 in the morning. The entrance fee was three halfpence plus a penny for bag of peanuts. The pictures were always Westerns, mainly serials, which ensured that the kids would always try to return the following Saturday. The toilet at the front of the cinema was in constant use. However, every time the large door from the interior of the cinema was opened to reach the outside toilet, a large black shadow would move across the screen, followed by whistles and shouts, calling out to the luckless kids to shut that bloody door! Invariably fights would break out at the back of the cinema and the able adult manager would chuck out all the troublemakers, whilst other kids would try and sneak back into the cinema through the door by the toilets.

The local police were treated with a great deal of suspicion by many of the poorer families of Islington. Generally, the local Bobby on the beat, nicknamed by us kids, 'The Rosser', was normally acceptable. He would keep an eye on us kids and we would either get good telling off or a clip round the ear, particularly if he caught us lighting fires in Dowrey Street to cook our spuds or for playing football in the main roads.

Anything else in blue would find a blind silence from the families while making inquiries for any reason. Considering that many boys from the district had fathers in prison, usually Pentonville, it did away with any public response to major crimes. There was a great deal of unemployment generally and the low wages turned ordinary people into petty thieves. Society at the same time did little to help. Men lined up for hours or walked miles to find work, any kind of work. My own eldest brother Pat was out of work for over two years, and he was one of thousands throughout the country. A great number of the boys I was at school with, including many I came into contact with in Islington, started off as small petty thieves and over the years never could get away from the habit, eventually being sent to borstals, which were the breeding grounds for more serious crimes, as the boys entered adulthood. Living in the squalor of rooms in tenements, with brothers and sisters, sleeping four, five or even six to a bed, if one existed, if not, on the floor – which was the only alternative – did little to expand the mind.

I was extremely fortunate; my father had a job. He worked hard, drank very little and always had an eye for business, buying and selling anything he honestly came by. I always had clean clothes and a clean bed.

At the time, I was too young to understand, but the poverty bred violence. Some men who managed to get some work, would often gravitate towards the public house on Friday nights, get drunk to blot out the misery of the hovels they lived in and the debts they owed for rent and to the money lenders. Other men turned to crime, inevitably being caught, and sent to prison for long terms, their wives and children trying to survive on national assistance. There was no escape from the poverty. Some boys, when they were old enough, ran away to sea, others just ran away never to return home. For the girls, no escape, unless they went on the 'Game' and then it was a gay life or a short one. Often, instead, they would stay at home bringing up their younger brothers and sisters while their mother was inside for thieving.

Friday and Saturday nights were often nights of violence. I was outside the Prince of Wales public house at the corner of Lofting Road and the Caley, with some mates, when two men fighting came out through the pub doors both streaming with blood, as other men were attempting to separate them. Eventually they fell into the gutter in Lofting Road – one underneath, one on top – both holding the tops of quart beer bottles by the neck and trying to stab each other.

On another occasion, in the Eclipse public house on Barnsbury Road, two men and their wives, fought in the bar with jagged broken glasses and then came out into the street and continued to fight, before being separated by other customers. The police on these occasions would carefully wait until the fiercest part of the fighting was over before they appeared and after some first aid treatment, the fighters would be warehoused in a police cell at the station and charged with drunkenness the following morning.

When the council were resurfacing Barnsbury Road us kids would build small round forts from the chunks of the tarmac road and in no time we were attacked by the kids from Gainsford Street, which was at the back of one side of Barnsbury Road, crossed at one end by Pulteney Street and at the other by Richmond Road. Their attacks became quite serious as we tried to repulse them. The kids from Gainsford Street would encourage the kids from Alma Grove and Pulteney Street to join them. We would then call on kids from other streets to support us and, before long, a massive gang fight was in progress. It was possible for this situation to go on for days before a truce was called, particularly if the kids from another part of Islington began to invade our streets, then previous opponents from Gainsford Street and Hemingford Road would join us in Barnsbury Road and take on the invaders.

As an alternative to fighting, homemade scooters began to appear on the streets. Simple to make and very easy to fall to bits. The main parts were two pieces of flat wood. Each piece had a V-shape cut in one end, the other had piece of broom stick nailed at the end. Four screw eyes were obtained, two of which were screwed into one of the pieces of wood, whilst the V-shaped piece would have block of wood nailed vertically at the opposite end. A large nail or long bolt would be inserted, securing the two pieces of wood together by passing through the four more eyes. The scooter was then taking shape, but wheels were now needed. This required two metal ball races which could be purchased from car breakers for a few pennies. The ball bearings would be roughly 4 to 5 inches in circumference and a wooden axle was pushed through the centre and nailed in between the V in the horizontal piece of wood. The other bearing was secured in the same manner to the bottom of the vertical piece of wood.

The wooden scooters varied in size and design, according to the funds available. Some boys had improved their scooters by installing a piece of rubber tyre on the base of the scooter at the rear, which by use of the foot could be pushed onto the ball bearing wheel to act as a brake. Later on the more adventurous boys would construct a box and, with additional ball races, would turn the scooter into a sidecar version.

Certainly, during the school holidays, these machines were put to good use, although the noise of several scooters clattering along the pavements caused quite a racket. The obvious place for a race between us kids was from the top end of Richmond Road, all downhill, taking our lives in our hands, crossing Hemingford Road and Matilda Street until, if still in one piece, the winner reached the Caley at the bottom. Inevitably these homemade scooters would come apart many times as the nails holding the wheels broke away from the main structure, with hair raising results.

On one occasion, two brothers in a scooter with sidecar chose to try out their new creation down Richmond Road. Everything went well until they reached Alma Grove, when a motor van backed out into Richmond Road. In trying to avoid the boy, the driver backed into a brick wall which collapsed, knocking down a ladder up which a house painter was working. The painter slid across two sets of houses on his ladder before coming to rest in a privet hedge, covered in the paint he was hanging onto. The boys careered on down the hill and in trying to slow down, the sidecar ball bearings were wrenched from the base of the car, causing the brother on the scooter to career across Hemingford Road, finishing up in someone's front garden. The brother still seated in the sidecar hanging on for grim death, managed to turn the corner and slid out of his wooden contraption into a newly deposited pile of horse shit. After this nerve-racking experience, our scooter activity stopped for some time.

The house I lived in, No. 162 Barnsbury Road, Islington, was like many of the houses in the road, being a three-storied property built before the 1900s. The only difference was that it had a shop at the road level. The whole property was owned by the Times Laundry Co., and my parents rented the basement and the rooms on the first floor, the top floor being let to a married couple by the name of Maynard. The entrance to 162 was through large red door with a round black enamel handle, set in the centre of the door. When this was opened there was another front door which led into passage with a high ceiling and brown embossed wallpaper, and at the end of the passage were two flights of stairs leading on to two rooms.

The room at the front, which had a veranda over the roof of the shop, was my parents' bedroom and because it was used as a parlour at Christmas, contained a double bed, three-piece suite, plus in front of each window, a cane table with the inevitable aspidistra. At the rear, the other room was my sister's bedroom. Both rooms were lit by gas.

On the ground floor a further staircase led down to the basement level. In the front was a large living room, but it was dark because only one small window faced out on to a wrought iron grille to the front of the road. Being below ground one single gas lamp needed to be on continuously to light the room. At the rear was a scullery with a stone floor and a door at the end of the room which led out to the lavatory. To go into the backyard, which was all concrete, one climbed the stairs to street level where a door opened onto the backyard. In the large basement living room, there were two single beds in which my two elder brothers slept, whilst I slept on a bed-chair. This room was also used as the living room and all our meals were eaten there. Apart from a coal fire boiler in the scullery, which was used to boil water for the weekly wash, the only form of heating came from the open fireplace in the adjoining living room.

No bathroom existed, but a large, galvanized bath which was normally kept hung on a nail on the wall of the backyard, was brought in on Friday nights to enable the family to take a bath. The water was heated on the black gas cooker or in the scullery boiler.

Looking back, I find it incredible to understand now my mother managed, with such little facilities, to feed six of us and keep us clean, but she did. Even with all the disadvantages of the living conditions, my home was certainly better than most, but my eyesight suffered from the inefficient light that the living room of 162, provided. This brought about the unavoidable eye test at school and the use of glasses. The fact that I was made to wear glasses was another cause of a great deal of embarrassment, particularly when I was without fail called 'four-eyes'.

Therefore, whenever the opportunity arose, I discarded the spectacles, or even said I had lost them. In any case I managed to do without them, certainly until I was summoned for another eye test.

As 162 was next door to the Eclipse public house on one side and a greengrocer's shop on the other, I was always intrigued by the noise and conversation that flowed from the pub. The greengrocer's shop kept open until late in the evenings, winter and summer. The owners, Gorrods, had a horse-drawn, covered van, which went to market to get supplies but was a mainly used on the greengrocer's round, calling on the different streets and dining rooms. Next to the Eclipse public house was a butcher shop which was next to Holland's fish shop. This stayed open until almost midnight and did good trade, especially as the average order was 'Tuppeny' and 'Pennyworth'. Dick Holland worked in the shop with his wife and young daughter, who was a year or two older than me. The daughter's problem ways the same. Whenever she went out with boys, they complained that she smelt of fried fish. Endless boys took her to the pictures, but only once.

The shop next to the fish shop had been used for various trades but was now a café. Most of its clientele seemed to be small time thieves and villains, plus a few old boxers, past their prime. The adjoining shop was a sweetshop owned by a Mr and Mrs Morris, who had a daughter called Lilly, who was my age. Two other shops completed the parade, one being a shoe repairer's called Johnson, who had two sons of school age and the last shop was a grocer's called Lights.

Although it seems far-fetched in today's world, I can recall, quite vividly, watching two men in their thirties, accompanied by a barrel organ and dressed as women, their faces made up, although the five o'clock shadow was very obvious, dancing in the road outside the Eclipse, in an effort to collect pennies from the patron of the pub. Even as a small boy, I felt a great shame and embarrassment for those men who were forced to make a spectacle of themselves in order to beg for pennies outside pubs in the streets of Islington.

During this period of my life, I remember a general election taking place. The respective candidates would tour the streets and set up their platforms at the corner of various roads. Usually, this would consist of a wooden orange or apple box from which the speaker would address the local residents. A complete contrast to today's halls with election agents and party officials to protect the political speaker during their speeches. They never failed to draw a large crowd but us boys would often follow the speaker from street to street as he extolled the excellence of his party and promised what they would do, if only the voters would vote for him. Heckling was always rife and on a number of occasions the candidate and his helpers would be forced to abandon their platform and run for safety as violence erupted.

I don't recall any speaker having a microphone so he had to have a good voice and be very quick on his feet, so as not to be hit by the assortment of missiles which came his way, if the crowd took a dislike to him or his party. If us boys knew in advance of particular speaker coming to Barnsbury Road or adjacent streets, to hold his meeting, we would visit Chapel

Street and collect all the rotten fruit we could find, to give to the adults, or even have a go ourselves when the comments of the political speaker were at odds with the local politics. Many a speaker found himself a target for well-sized missiles, simply because he had a cultured voice or was an existing member of the day's present government.

November the 5th was always awaited with great excitement, whatever pennies could be obtained by doing odd jobs etc., would be used to buy bangers of any variety, remembering that these were a halfpenny each. Depending on how much each boy could contribute, quite a number could be obtained. We would put the bangers on the ground with a dustbin lid over the top or put them in darkened alleyways, where courting couples frequented, and the bangers always created noise and havoc. It wasn't the kind of prank to get involved in unless you were fairly quick on your feet and could run. If you didn't have the mobility, you would get a good clout round your ears from irate lovers or adults living nearby.

The most daring thing us boys did was to watch for men leaving the Lamb public house at the bottom of Thornhill Road, intent on using the gentlemen's urinal, which stood in all its glory at the bottom of Barnsbury Road, in front of the gardens, near the top of Richmond Road. This building was of Victorian design, made of cast iron, dirty green in colour and as a recent addition, a glass roof had been provided. On bonfire nights as two or three men left the Lamb to relieve themselves, we would wait until the men were halfway to the urinal and then rush into the back of it, leaving a lighted banger.

We would then seat ourselves on the kerb on the opposite side of the road. The timing was not always good but generally the men would be about halfway through relieving themselves, when the banger would explode, lighting up the inside of the urinal. The result was always the same following the blue flash which we could see through the glass roof. The men would run out into the road in varying states of undress, whilst we sat on the kerb opposite, acting as if it was nothing to do with us. Nevertheless, it didn't take long before they realized who the culprits were and we would take off in all directions, at great speed, resembling together later, until further men left the pub and made their way unsuspectingly into the green urinal. The procedure was always on the same basis but, invariably, one of our gang, slightly slow off the mark, would be the recipient of a clout round the ear from one of the victims.

My father was a hard working man but also shrewd and when a garage became vacant in Clement Street at the top of Thornhill Road and Lofting Road, he rented the property, which could garage between nine and ten cars and/or vans. The profit he made from this investment helped to give our family a better life than most. Uneducated, his knowledge of money was second to none and as my eldest brother Pat had taught him to drive a car, it wasn't long before he did a deal and acquired a second-hand Renault motor car. The price of used cars was a little different to present day car values. The Renault cost my father, two pounds, ten shillings. One Saturday lunch time, I was duly despatched by him to buy a tin of chocolate brown paint. Whenever my father painted anything, he always used chocolate brown paint. I obtained this from the small oil shop round the corner in Cloudesley Road.

Armed with the paint, my father began by painting the off side of the car, facing away from the kerb. The original colour of the car was blue. He set to the task with great relish, no rubbing down, no undercoat, just straight on with his beloved chocolate brown, and he had just completed the one side when my mother called him for dinner, after which he fell asleep on the couch. The sequel to his painting the car came when he awoke, went out to inspect his handiwork and discovered that a cart distributing sand and gravel onto the newly laid tarmac road, had thrown the sand and gravel onto the painted side. It resembled a large piece of sand-paper.

The car was quickly sold one evening to one of the new-found rich, who, fortunately for my father, failed to notice the sand-papered side effect as he drove the car away. However, the following Saturday saw my father with another of his fifty-shilling motor cars, which, irrespective of its colour, would be transformed into chocolate brown.

It was in this series of motor cars, which never cost more than three pounds, ten shillings, that my parents took me for several weekends in the summer to Southend and nearby Shoeburyness. If however, my father was approached by someone local in Islington as to whether he would sell his present model, providing a reasonable profit could be made, then the deal was done. I have lost count as to the number and makes of car he bought and sold up to the outbreak of the war. All I remember is that we rarely had the same car two weeks running. The only thing my father needed to establish was that it was a good runner.

The opportunity to be able to be in the country and the seaside was certainly a bonus for me during the summer, after a winter spent in Islington.

On some Sunday nights, if my father had had a good week, moneywise, he would take my mother out for a drink, usually to the Royal Oak, at the top of Thornhill Road. I would tag along and be rewarded with a penny bag of Smith's crisps with the famous blue paper containing salt. On such a night, I would sit outside the pub and watch two, or sometimes three, horse-drawn vehicles, bringing the carcasses from the abattoir, situated by the old Indian Market on their way down Thornhill Road, onto Liverpool Road and the Angel, then along Goswell Road, finishing up at Springfield Market. The vehicles were usually pulled by two magnificent carthorses, although, if it was a heavy load, four horses would be used.

The vans had open sides with heavy canvas blinds along the sides of the vehicles. The noise of the steel rimmed wheels could be heard before they got to the Royal Oak and the noise continued for long time as they trundled past, on their way to Liverpool Road, leading towards the city.

As the year was ending and the new year was upon us, I was, in that April of 1936, twelve years of age and, even at that age, I sensed that things were changing. My eldest brother Pat had acquired a radio, operated by a dry battery and an accumulator, which needed to be changed every two or three days.

Even at my age I could understand the day-to-day news. Civil war had broken out in Spain and in Islington a great many young men in their late teens and twenties were joining the International Brigade and leaving for Spain to fight fascism.

Whether it was their politics or the money, a great many elder brothers of boys I was at school with, joined this brigade just to get away from being out of work and living in tenements.

Political meetings became more aggressive, and people seemed to be taking more notice of what the speakers were saying. Several meetings held in Islington by Sir Oswald Mosley's Blackshirts erupted into street violence. The targets were the Jewish families in Islington and the scene was quite frightening to us boys as these Blackshirts, marching, over six abreast and with more than a hundred in the group, would smash the windows of Jewish owned shops and businesses and then attack the individual Jewish families.

I remember sometime later that year, taking Lilly Morris, the daughter of Jewish parents, who owned the sweetshop, into my house as the Blackshirts marched from Thornhill Road into Barnsbury Road one evening and began to smash up the sweetshop. The whole Morris family was terrified, particularly as these Blackshirts were often local men from Islington and the surrounding districts, dressed up to emulate the new Nazi regime beginning to stir in Germany.

Though I didn't realize it then, it was indeed a wind of change that was blowing from Europe across Great Britain and the men who had been unemployed for years, suddenly discovered that powerful, wealthy and important interests needed these men to further their politics cause. Uniforms of one kind or another plus some food and few shillings in their pockets to spend, meant they were fair game to their political masters. Tragically, many men who left for Spain, believing they were fighting for freedom, sadly either returned home wiser men or lost their lives for a dream.

Back at St Thomas' Boys' School – mainly because I moved from the headmaster's class into the top class – school life began to take on a different meaning for me. Basically, school work was the same but because Mr Taylor (Tas) the teacher, had a softer approach for many of us boys who had moved up in class, he seemed to sense my own particular apprehension.

'Tas' Taylor, about thirty-five years of age, married with three children of his own, had an advantage over his colleagues, he had a degree, a BA. As I progressed under his teaching, I had no idea, and I am sure that Tas could not have known what impact he made on me at twelve years of age, and to a much greater degree, throughout my adult life.

Tas Taylor born at Cirencester, and a Gloucesterman throughout his life, was the son of a farmer who chose to take up teaching and of all places, finished up at St Thomas', Islington. He was fairly tall and with steel grey bushy hair, very active and fit. There is no doubt that he was admired by the majority of boys who were fortunate to have him as a teacher during their school life.

He had the unique gift or being able to hold the attention of a classroom of boys, with his wonderful stories, which in a special way, he could turn into a lesson. I was fortunate to have direct descendants of Shelley and Swinerton in my class and Tas Taylor encouraged them to such an extent that Swinerton won a scholarship and went on to greater things, whilst Shelley, an accomplished cartoonist, became quite successful.

Although Tas Taylor was essentially a cricketer and always prepared to extol the merits of Wally Hammond, the famous Gloucestershire cricketer, it was a surprise to many that his second love was football. He was also a sports master, and we had a school football team entered in the local school league which played a match against another school every Saturday morning. It one a great surprise to find my name included in the St Thomas' team. Tas had not asked me to play or whether I wanted to play, he had just observed that I was a fairly good runner and liked to kick a ball around. He put me in the position of outside right and I couldn't believe my eyes when I actually scored the winning goal of the match.

This particular successful event was a real new beginning for me because as I progressed with Tas Taylor's help and encouragement I began to come out of my shell, not only in sports activities but in general school work. In football I was very successful, never missing a match until I left school. I was very proficient in running and other events. Of all things, Tas Taylor obtained a darts board and because he always arrived about an hour before school began, I would arrive at school at about 08.00 hours and Tas and I would play darts for about an hour.

I think the only disappointment I created for him was when taking the exams with one of my school friends, a boy named Arthur Lear at Richard Street School Examination Centre. I, for a somewhat rash reason, failed the exam because my pal Arthur's parents were fairly poor and wanted him to go right to work after he left school, rather than win a scholarship. He decided to fail the paper and I did likewise. Some weeks later, I remember getting a hell of telling off from an irate Tas

Taylor. At the time I felt ashamed that I had let him down but, nevertheless, he never mentioned it again and our friendship grew as I got older.

Although I was improving, I still had this unfortunate speech impediment and when Tas arranged for us boys to visit the Old Vic, to see Shakespeare's *As You Like It*, our headmaster 'Kipper' Roe decided to put on our own play at school. He chose *Macbeth* and, for obvious reasons, when the parts were being handed out, I was not included. I remember Tas saying to me, with a wicked glint in is eye, 'If we put you in the play, everybody will have gone home before you can speak your lines'. As fate would have it, the boy due to play Angus, went down with influenza the day the play was to be performed. So, as there was no alternative boy to play the part, other than me, with a great deal of reluctance on the part of the headmaster, I was called upon to take that part in Shakespeare's great play.

To everyone's surprise, including my own, I never stuttered or stammered throughout my whole performance. Tas Taylor never let me forget my faultless performance in the play and after the many years since, I am still extremely grateful to him and admire him greatly for the time, patience and sensitivity he gave to me. I remember always the wisdom he passed onto me when I was a young lad and he was a wonderful, understanding man when he told us boys that if we ever went to Cheltenham we would see an avenue lined with trees either side of the road and lovely green parks, as opposed to the derelict and grimy property and streets in which we lived and played.

At the time, Cheltenham seemed to me personally, so far away that I would never ever have the opportunity of seeing the tree lined road. However, without being aware that the black clouds of the Second World War were gathering in Europe, in some short five years after I left school in 1938, I was to have the time and opportunity to remember Tas Taylor's word picture that he drew for me of Cheltenham, when I was twelve, as during the war I had occasion to visit Tas's town.

It was during 1936 – perhaps due to the impending uncertainty of the situation in Europe – that more work became available and the unemployment in Islington and surrounding areas eased slightly. I continued at school, and I became proficient in my school work and in football due mainly to the understanding of Tas Taylor.

Outside of school I became friends with the boys from Barnsbury Road again and everyone became interested in bicycles. My father acquired a second-hand bike and my two older brothers spent hours repairing it before I was able to try it out along Barnsbury Road. On my first attempt, not having ridden a bike before, I crashed into some railings and almost went down into the basement of a nearby house. However, no damage done, and I persisted until I became quite proficient. The only disadvantage was that I got a sore backside, but in time the situation eased.

Several new families moved into the road, so we had quite a gang of boys who plagued a newsagent and tobacconist at the top of Richmond Road, by the name of Charlie Travers, 'Mad Charlie' we called him. When we decided to have a bonfire in Dowrey Street, we would pinch all Mad Charlie's old papers from outside his shop. We would rush by his shop, grab a few handfuls, and run like hell, being chased by him. He never caught us although we were always careful not to use his shop for a few days.

A new boy came to St Thomas' the name Ron Bowyer and by a strange coincidence he was not only the same age as me but had exactly the same birthday. His family had moved into a block of new flats built at the top end of Barnsbury Road and Copenhagen Street. These flats had been built on the site of a number of tenements which were demolished to make way for this block of flats, which were several storeys high. Unfortunately, the bricks from the demolished tenements had been used in the building of the new flats and in no time at all the flat became infested with the red coat brigade (bedbugs). This necessitated all the flats having to be fumigated.

Ron Bowyer and I became friends and I discovered he had a natural talent as a cartoonist and gave great delight to all of us at school with his endless cartoons. After I left school I lost contact with Ron Bowyer but his intention was to join Webster, the cartoonist of the *Evening News* and I am sure he gave pleasure to many people.

The cinema began to interest us boys, particularly during the holiday period. The number of these gave a varied choice. At the Angel, Islington, next to the Lyons' Corner House, was the Angel Cinema, originally a tram depot. Across the road and almost opposite at the bottom end of Liverpool Road was the Empire. This was a favourite, principally because of the price up in the 'Gods' (balcony). It was three pence, before 15.00 hours and four pence after 16.00 hours. The Empire had an illustrious history. Before it became a cinema it was a music hall and before that a cinema.

I can recall my mother telling me that as a small girl she had watched the horse-drawn carriages bringing the well-dressed patrons to the theatre every evening. Us boys liked the Empire because during the film or in the interval we would drop the orange peel or banana skins from the fruit we had pinched from the stalls in Chapel Street Market, over the balcony onto the customers below. This invariably caused the cinema commissionaire to charge upstairs to the balcony to try and catch us chucking our rubbish over the top. Sometimes he was successful, and would throw us all out, but because he was such a big man we would dodge him and hide in the gents until he returned downstairs. Further along the high pavement in the Upper Street and near to the Collins' Music Hall, Islington Green, was the flea pit called the Empress (later the Rex). This again was good for a Saturday morning event, particularly with Westerns and serials.

Along further, almost next door to the police station in the Upper Street and near to the town hall was the Lido, later a petrol filling station. Being next door to the police station, this cinema was a little too refined for us.

About this time a new cinema opened at the top end of the Caledonian Road, again next door to the police station, opposite Caley Underground station. In the beginning it was called the Mayfair, its name being changed after the war to Essoldo. If we were able to con an adult to take us in, we could watch two films and a band show. The difficulty with this cinema was that they wouldn't allow us ruffians in, so unless we could persuade an adult to take, say two of us in, it would be hard for us to gain admission.

Spinning tops became our next craze, mostly wooden heavy-duty ones, which we would whip up and down the pavements of Barnsbury Road. We discovered, by drawing patterns on the head of the top, we could create different designs.

One of the highlights of the year was the party which was put on for us kids in Barnsbury Road by the baker's shop at the corner of Pulteney Street and Barnsbury Road. The owners would clear their cellar of flour and give us kids a real blow out, with sandwiches, jellies and trifles, something we all looked forward to with great longing.

Another delight for those boys who had a penny, was to visit a small fish shop called Joe Morris's in adjacent Gainsford Street. For a penny we could obtain three scallops (round slices of potato covered in batter and fried). To us boys it was sheer heaven with loads of salt and vinegar. I have never, ever had potatoes cooked like Joe Morris could cook them. In fact I have never had them or anything like them since I left Islington during the war.

During the summer months I would go to meet my father returning from his place of work, when I was often rewarded with a penny for sweets. Now that my father had his rented garage in Clements Street at the top of Thornhill Road and Lofting Road, he would often call at the garage on his way home to check that everything was in order. Most of the kids who lived either is Clements Street or adjacent to it were very much the same as my friends in Barnsbury Road. However, near my father's garage was a small shop in which the owner carried out a bicycle business. All the bikes were second hand and of various sizes and makes. Very few boys owned a bike so it was a great deal of fun to hire a bike for the sum of three pence per half hour or sixpence for the hour.

It was, therefore, hilarious to watch as two or three boys would contribute a penny each to make up the required three pence and hire a bike between them for half an hour. They would take it in turn to ride to bike round the streets, and well over the allotted half hour, by a dozen or more boys. The owner of the bikes would rush round the nearby streets trying to catch the boys in an effort to return the bikes to his shop. Many evenings he would spend nearly all his time until dusk before he managed to regain the last of his bikes. Strange as it may seem, this situation never changed, as night after night, the boys would repeat the previous evening activities and carry on riding the hired bikes over the allotted time, with the owner always in hot pursuit, trying to collect his property.

Life was never boring, even in the school holidays, our little gang would always think up an idea for making money. On some days we would pay a visit to Chapel Street Market where we would try to collect all the wooden boxes, take them to Dowrey Street and break them into small sticks, tie them with string and then go along to houses in Brooksby Street, Park Street and Barnsbury Road, where we hoped to sell the firewood to occupants.

As the winter nights came along, we would look forward to the circus provided by Bertram Mills, which was held at the agricultural hall which faced onto the Upper Street near Islington Road and extended right through to Liverpool Road at the rear. This always caused a surge of boys from all around Islington to converge and form a very long queue, from the entrance to the hall in the Upper Street, round the corner and up the side, reaching to the rear in Liverpool Road. This usually began on Saturdays as early as 08.00 hours in the morning, from the first week in December until late into January. The entrance fee for boys was usually sixpence, which allowed you into the hall. To enter the inner section, where the circus took place, would cost anything from two shillings and six pence upwards.

This being far more than any of us could afford, meant that we would wander around the hall looking at the animals and, in the confined conditions, the smell was awful. The only highlight would be when the trapeze artists began their act and we could see them performing if we stood back against the walls of the hall.

During 1937 a great many people seemed to be leaving Barnsbury Road and the surrounding area as many of the houses and tenements had 'To Let' signs outside them. I had my thirteenth birthday and got my first pair of long trousers. These were in a lovely dark grey material although for some time I felt very self-conscious when I wore them.

Most weekends that summer my father would go away to Shoeburyness in Essex and did in fact purchase a small caravan. As the caravan was sited in an orchard, fresh fruit was abundant. We travelled away to the caravan most Saturday afternoons and stayed over until Sunday evening, when we returned home. I thoroughly enjoyed the opportunity of being completely in the country and at the same time had the pleasure of the seaside a mile or so away.

Returning to school after the summer break, football began to become important to me and our school team played quite a number of friendly matches with other teams, so much so that I drifted away from the boys in Barnsbury Road and spent the majority of evenings in and around Everilda Street, Matilda Street, Thornhill Square and the Caledonian Road (the Caley).

On the occasion of a school league match, the games were played on the football pitches at Finsbury Park and usually began by kicking off at 11.00 hours in the morning. We would change into our football kit in school and then walk down to the Caley to catch the tram to Finsbury Park. Fortunately for the school, we had a benefactor in the name of Connell, a local butcher, with his shop in a small parade of shops at the corner of the Caley and Copenhagen Street, almost opposite the Milford Haven public house. Mr Connell had made an arrangement that he would pay all our tram fares to and from Finsbury Park, which proved to be a very generous gift.

It was during the latter part of 1937 that my dad decided to move house, partly because my elder brother and sister had both recently got married. I recall, with a certain amount of hilarity but also clouded with nostalgia, that my father made his decision one autumn night. He turned up outside No. 162 Barnsbury Road with an empty coal cart and began to load our precious item of furniture onto the cart. Because we had large coal cellars, I found that I was given the task of shovelling the coal into bags and carrying them upstairs to the cart. Everything was piled high and while my mother walked behind with an assortment of suitcases containing the bed linen etc., I, similarly loaded, followed the cart along to Richmond Road, on to Liverpool Road, and turned into a road called College Cross, No. 15.

Because it was dark the entire operation was hilarious from start to finish, although at No. 15 the house was lit by electricity as opposed to the gaslight at our previous abode. Everything was strange and the furniture had to be unloaded and handed over some railings, down into the airey [a prefabricated structure], where there were two further rooms at street level.

Most of the small furniture was easily handled and in a short time some resemblance of order began to appear. The result was that my father took a saw and cut the settee in two halves. Having taken in the two halves and placed them in the position he required, he called upon me to pass him some 6-inch nails and a hammer, whereupon he proceeded to nail the two halves together again. Having completed the job and discovering that all the furniture and effects were now installed in No. 15, he called to my mother, 'Everything's in, put the kettle on Flo and make a cup of tea.' At the same time he sat down on the settee, which promptly collapsed and being a man of 15 or 16 stone, he was on his back like a beetle. My mother had mild hysterics and I took off into the kitchen, fearing his wrath. Later on, more repairs were carried out on the offending settee and order began to prevail.

I recall my first sight of television came one evening, when about four of us boys, riding around the streets at the bottom of Richmond Road, decided to get some chips from local fish shop in Bingfield Street. We parked our bikes alongside the kerb and entered the fish shop. Set in one corner was a small cabinet which looked like a radio, but I could see a small glass window and, moving across, the small figure of women dancer in ballet dress. As the picture was in black and white the contrast was marvellous. For several weeks whenever we were riding out in the streets, us boys would always finish up at the corner of Bingfield Street and Bemerton Street. I am sure the turnover of the shop must have increased many times because of the television set on show in the shop.

It was about this time that girls from our school, St Thomas's, who lived round the Caley, began to feature in our lives. Although I had many friends among the boys at school, a great many of these boys lived in other streets which led off from Copenhagen Street and the Caley. This meant that they often kept to their own streets, but because I began to frequent the bottom end of Matilda Street, where it joined the bottom of Richmond Road, a little group of boys from the nearby streets began to meet most evenings on the corner, quite close to Thornhill Square. I can recall that there was Bobby Reardon and Bobby Chinnock from Thornhill Square, George Storror and from Pulteney Street close to my former house in Bansbury Road, 'Bunter' Tibbles, also from Pulteney Street, and, some two years older than most of us and at work, and me from College Cross.

Our presence seemed to attract some of the local girls, the names of whom come easily to mind: Doris Skinner from Richmond Road, also Jean Sibley whose parents gave her wonderful birthday parties, Joyce Sudley from Thornhill Square, Iris Glazier, Doris Springate from Hemingford Road, Doris Stidder and Olive Popple, both from Matilda Street.

Olive, strange to relate, had been my girlfriend since she was seven and I was about nine and although now married to an old friend of mine from school, Freeman Kitchener, we are all still very good friends.

As bikes were still very much the craze in the lighter evenings, we would take a girl each on the crossbar of our bikes and go careering around Thornhill Square. I remember one occasion when Olive borrowed her sister's green racing bike and had a race with me but we went off in different directions. The result was a draw as when we both approached the finishing line, we crashed into one another, causing a great deal of laughter from the onlookers. Although only slight damage to the bikes and a few abrasions, Olive certainly proved she could ride a racing bike.

Christmas 1937 came around and as it was our first Christmas at 15 College Cross, most of our family decided to pay us a visit at our house, and rooms seemed to be continually invaded by boyfriends and girlfriends of my brother and sister, including friends of my married brother. How my mother coped, I have no idea, but on Christmas night a party began and went on until Boxing Day. It is strange to recall that this was the last occasion when our family and friends were all together at our family home.

I remember, with great nostalgia, my eldest brother Pat, dancing with my Gran (my mother's mother) round and round the living room floor. My Gran was a lovely lady but only about 4 feet 11 inches in height and at the end of the dance she was so dizzy that Pat, my brother, had to hold her up. Considering she was eighty years of age it was a wonder that she could stand at all. Nevertheless, she was game until the end, though after a glass of sherry my father and I had to escort her home to her little flat, nearby in Lonsdale Square.

The following morning, Boxing Day, she appeared at our house quite refreshed and ready for her dinner. Quite a lady, our Gran.

As I was now in my fourteenth year I, accompanied by my mother, was called upon to go before a panel of people at St Thomas' School whose sole purpose was to establish what kind of trade or profession I wished to take up on leaving school. This was a normal function in those days. It was quite formal and when my turn came it was established that I would leave school at the Easter recess in three months' time, April 1938, and as agreed by my parents that I would find my own job and go into an office in the City of London. The next three months seemed to drag but with football, bikes and girls, life progressed in an orderly fashion.

My father still continued to acquire various motor cars which he always repainted to his favourite chocolate brown colour and then promptly sold for a profit. As it was further for my mother to walk to the market at Chapel Street, I often went with her to help carry her shopping bags. This meant walking into Liverpool Road and along to the end, where it joined the Upper Street.

Over the years, I have been back along the route in Chapel Market although it in often said that time diminishes the memory, I find that once in the market, certain individuals names always come to mind. When I went with my mother on Fridays or Saturdays, invariably the so-called 'Prince Monolulu' would be calling out in his own fashion, which was unique,

'I gotta horse'. The fact that he was a horse racing tipster, that he was black and always dressed in his own colourful garments, added to his charm. He was part of the happy, bustling crowd of busy people enjoying the market scene. He was part of the picture I can recall with a great deal of sadness, the characters and stallholders who formed a part of a weekend's shopping in Chapel Street market in the Islington I knew but they have long gone.

The lady who stood halfway down the market, rain or shine, calling out, 'Get your Pine Disinfectant', the stallholders selling greengrocery, the Bernadin Bros. – these brothers were at school with my brother at nearby Richard Street School, the lady who sold sarsaparilla on the corner of Chapel Street and White Conduit Street, the Hutchinsons, Redknapps etc., Sainsbury's grocer shop on the corner of Baron Street and Chapel Street, and Chas Phillips another grocer. The stall selling fish with tanks containing live eels, the various butchers standing outside their respective shop, dressed in their blue and white striped aprons and straw boaters, yelling at the top of their voices to overcome the noise of the crowds, 'Buy! Buy!' The Chapel House public house, the hot chestnut stands, Manzi's pie and eel shop. The baker's shop where you could buy thirteen donuts (a baker's dozen) for a shilling. The In and Out shop where you could buy all modes of clothing for men, women and children, very cheaply. My father's pet name for a suit purchased from this establishment was 'Nottingham Hosiery'. He also quipped, 'Buy a suit three times your size, and out in the rain and when it dries it will fit you.' Woolworths, next door, which proudly, boasted nothing over three pence and sixpence, where I and many others during the pre-war years played the game of rushing into the store through the Chapel Street entrance, nicking something and running like hell out of the other side of the store, through the Liverpool Road entrance.

I remember with slight embarrassment and part sadness, Sidney Smith's, the pawnbrokers at the corner of Liverpool Road and the Upper Street, where, as a very young boy, before I went to school, I stood in the Liverpool Road entrance of the pawnbrokers with my mother, who on frequent Monday mornings would pawn some item – either her wedding ring or something from our home – for enough money to able to buy food for the evening meal. She would return to the pawnbrokers on the Friday or Saturday when my father gave her the shopping money to redeem the item she had pawned, repaying the money plus the 1 per cent interest charged. My father never knew and never found out how my mother always managed to put a meal on the table.

Ironically it was many years after the war, when I was no longer living in Islington, that I suddenly realized that the side door in Liverpool Road was indeed the entrance to the pawnbroker, where I queued with my mother on Mondays. I was too young to understand but years later I felt sick, not with shame, but with regret in the knowledge that along with great many women around the district, my mother had been forced to stand in line and pawn her possessions to buy food. A more pleasant aspect was that next door to Sidney Smith's was Nick Golds', the sweet shop, where you could buy a pound of assorted excellent chocolates for six pence.

The Lyons' Corner House at the corner of the Upper Street and Pentonville Road by the traffic lights was where, as I grew older, many of budding romances began and ended. Next door, the Saxone Shoe Company where my brother Ernie bought me one evening (when I had been at work only a few weeks), my first pair of new shoes. They cost eighteen shillings, I recall I paid him back a shilling a week from my wages, an episode in my life I never forgot. My father's comment to my brother at the time was, 'He'll kick them out in a fortnight.' To prove him wrong I walked as lightly as I could for months.

I still have the memory of being taken as a youngster by my father on Sundays to Chapel Street where the 'Trotters', with their stalls of second-hand clothing, shoes, boots, etc., offered their wares. Having to try on second-hand shoes in assorted colours, inevitably too big in size, but father would buy a pair, telling me to put newspaper in the toes, and of his favourite end to my objections: 'You'll grow into them'. These events in my life regarding second-hand clothes and shoes, I hated and have never forgotten.

In later years when the opportunity has arisen and I have visited Chapel Street Market, the atmosphere has completely changed. The crowds are there but nowhere approaching the numbers that shopped in the market in pre-war days. A few old hands still remain but mostly sons, daughter or even grandchildren carry on the trade that their forebears began many years before.

One old friend who was also a friend of my brother Ernie, still pursues his business in the lower part of Chapel Street. He is Ernie Hollister, who, together with his charming wife, still sells crabs, shrimps, winkles, etc. on his stall. In his day he was a very able boxer along with his brother Ally Hollister who ran a pub in Chapel Street. As Ernie said to me on our last meeting, and I quote: 'The old days are gone, along with the people, the market's finished.' Sadly, that fact is true, but it was for many who grew up round the market, a highlight in the somewhat drab existence that prevailed in Islington before the war.

To end this sad reflection on the Chapel Street Market area, I must recall a man who was a great friend of my father and the many stallholders and people who lived around this part of Islington. Tom Treacy, married with two children, carried on his business of funeral director. My father, on many occasions, drove the horse-drawn hearse, sometimes with two black Arab stallions or four horses and even eight horses drawing the hearse. Whenever a local family or a member of the stallholders in the market were bereaved, Tom Treacy carried out the arrangements for the funeral and burial of the deceased.

As a boy I heard my father tell many stories that involved Tom Treacy, one in particular comes to mind. On one occasion both my father and Tom Treacy were in a public house one lunchtime and in a glass cabinet on the bar were the usual pies, pasties and sausage rolls. Shortly before they left the bar Tom Treacy took a number of his business cards out of his waistcoat pocket and proceeded to insert each card into the top of each pie, pastie, etc. The fact that on it the cards read, 'Tom Treacy, Funeral Director', was not lost on the licensee, who was not amused by the incident.

Our two families became quite close, often spending weekends together in Shoeburyness, Essex. Tragically, Tom was killed near the Angel, Islington, during the early part of the war when, one night, he tried to extinguish an incendiary bomb dropped by German bombers and the incendiary exploded. To add to this, a few nights later, when his wife and daughter were sheltering in the safety of Lady Owen's School, nearby, both were killed by a German land mine that dropped on or near the school causing a great many civilian casualties. Thus, only the son was left to continue his late father's business.

Returning to my own last few weeks at school, I found that my personal thoughts were tinged with sadness for St Thomas's. The teachers had not only taught me the basic three Rs, but in the case of Tas Taylor, he has the foresight and ability to encourage a young boy to open his eyes to a wider horizon, both academically and to parts of the country and the world outside of the life and environment I knew in Islington.

I have always been extremely proud of being born a native of Islington and although before the turn of the century up to the present day, the district has had its ups and downs, I have at different times in my adult life, been asked whether, given my time over again, I would have wished to have been born in an up-market area. My answer has always been the same.

With the hindsight of years, perhaps I could have had a better crack of the whip academically, if I had gone to a grammar school or even university, but the street knowledge I gained as a boy, growing up in Islington, mixing with the many colourful characters who became part of my life, far exceeds a life that hypothetically might have been. I can also add that I was indeed fortunate in having the wisdom of my father, who incidentally, was uneducated, but overcame this difficulty. The love and affection of my mother, who gave me an understanding of a different kind, which has served me well.

Some two weeks before I left school at the Easter break, my mother and I and been to an employment agency in Broad Street, quite near Liverpool Railway Station, in the City of London. It turned out to be fortuitous in so much that I secured a position as office/messenger/tea boy at a company of watch makers.

I remember travelling on my own to Moorgate Street Chambers, in Moorgate Street, London, EC2. Presenting myself at the office of Messrs Moise Dreyfuss, situated with many other firms on the first floor of the chambers, I was shown into the luxurious office of Sylvain Dreyfuss, who conducted the interview. Later on I met his other brother Georges, both directors of the firm with the trademark of 'Rotary' watches. Through the atmosphere heavy with the aroma of expensive cigars, I was taken on an office boy, starting the following Monday morning.

Highly delighted and with the knowledge that I would be paid seventeen and six pence each week, less four pence National Health and Insurance contributions I went home feeling 10 feet tall.

Easter was early in 1938 and the school broke up mid-week, which meant I could start work the following Monday as arranged. Several of my school friends were also leaving at the same time, many joining the ranks of dead-end jobs as van boys, riding in the rear of vans, both horse-drawn as well as motor-drawn, ensuring that the goods in the vans were not stolen before they reached their destination. I had said goodbye to other friends and thanked Kipper Roe, our headmaster, and Robo Robinson, my teacher in earlier years, for their endeavours.

Then came the time to thank and wish goodbye to Tas Taylor, who not only educated me but whose knowledge and wisdom was to have such an impact on me and influence my thinking in later years. Tas Taylor wished me success in my employment and asked me to keep in touch. His parting words will always remain with me: 'Be yourself and observe the world around you'.

I met, as usual, the gang of boys and girls that evening, where we discussed the pros and cons of my new forthcoming employment.

On the Monday morning, bright and early, I left home to start my new job. I walked along the Upper Street and adjacent to the Islington Town Hall, waited in a small queue until the No. 43 bus came along and for a two pence fare, travelled along Upper Street and thence to Moorgate Street.

My first day consisted of being shown the ropes, so to speak, by an older man. This meant a marvellous education involving getting to know the City of London streets, walkways and major buildings. Depending on the volume of work, supplying new watches and returning watches that had been repaired to jewellers and wholesalers within the City area, was almost my daily task. This would usually begin by taking all the small packets and parcels to individual customers in places like Cheapside, Broad Street, Air Street, Hatton Garden, Clerkenwell Road, Holborn and Bishopsgate. When I returned to the office a mighty task faced me – the job of taking all the letters and small packets to the Post Office in nearby Fore Street. As most required to be registered I often found that after leaving the office with my two suitcases full of packets at around 17.00 hours I often never returned to the office until after 18.00, by which time the office cleaners were in full swing.

I had been employed for just one week when I was called into the office of Mr S. Dreyfuss. Fearing the worst, I was apprehensive. I was told that because I was still only thirteen years of age, I would have to go home wait a week and then rejoin the firm. I had overlooked the fact that although the school recess was early in April, I wasn't fourteen until my birthday on 26 April. The school authorities had in fact allowed me to leave school two weeks before I reach my fourteenth birthday. Everything was finally settled, and I rejoined the firm, although I have always stated that I began work when I was thirteen.

On my first pay day on Friday I duly received my wages, seventeen and sixpence less deduction of four pence. I gave the whole remaining amount to my mother and received two shillings pocket money and two shillings bus fare to and from work. As the fare to and from Moorgate Street amounted to four pence each day, I often left home early and walked the whole distance to my place of work and therefore saved two shillings bus fare.

At the time I felt extremely well off and considering that I could visit the cinema for just sixpence and, as I really enjoyed the films, I found I could often visit the cinema three times a week for one shilling and sixpence and still have money in my pocket.

I enjoyed my work as I was my own boss, more or less, when I was out in the City of London delivering my packets of watches. I took sandwiches for lunch and when the weather was fine I would take my lunch hour sitting on a park bench either in Finsbury Circus or more preferably on a seat near St Botolph's church in Bishopsgate and watch the men and women playing tennis in their lunch hour.

However, my walking to and from work and subsequent walking making my deliveries, had a dramatic effect on my shoes. Holes began to appear in the soles, so much so, that on days when it rained, I was forced to cut pieces of cardboard to replace the rain sodden inserts during the day.

As I was still meeting the boys and girls from around Matilda Street in the evening, it became a Friday night special to go to the newly opened Gaumont Cinema at the Nag's Head in Holloway. It held 1,000 people. Four or five of us kids would pay a shilling and three pence to go in the dress circle to watch two big films and, in the interval, a band show and cabaret lasting an hour.

This became a highlight for many Friday nights, with big, well-known bands such as Ambrose and his Orchestra with the vocalist a young Anne Shelton. Alternate weekends, ice hockey at Harringay Arena became the vogue for us, watching two teams mainly consisting of Canadian players in both teams chasing round the ice rink, knocking hell out of each other.

With money in my pocket, increased by some overtime, and a good bike which I was now using to go to work and make my deliveries, life was very heady, but the storm clouds were gathering in Europe. The talk of war was beginning to take over in many conversations. Many people were sceptical that war would ever break out, while men of my father's generation would quietly comment: 'I hope to God it never does, I remember the last lot.'

All of this was a long way off as far as I was concerned. To enjoy life was all that mattered to youngsters of my age group.

Olive and I were seeing much more of each other, and the other boys were pairing off with girlfriends. A cold winter preceded Christmas and the New Year bringing in 1939. There was more serious talk of war and Hitler, but people brushed such fears aside. 'Let's enjoy Christmas,' appeared to be the general idea.

I received a rise of two shillings and six pence which took me into the one pound a week bracket. I had never known anything like it as I was still earning another ten or fifteen shillings a week doing overtime on top of my one pound wages.

Unknown to my father, I began buying the odd packet of cigarettes, mostly at the weekends. I usually bought twenty Kensitas with an 'Extra four cigarettes for your friends' stuck on the outside of the packet!

With the coming of spring and the long nights, us boys began to use our bikes more and go further afield, travelling down into the East End of London and on one occasion riding through the Blackwall Tunnel, near Poplar. This proved to be a marvellous sensation as we sped down into the tunnel and freewheeled for a considerable distance and then discovered that we were drawn along the uphill side of the tunnel by suction, having only to pedal for a short distance out into nearby Greenwich.

We had all discussed the question of camping one weekend but nothing definite had been planned. However, George Storrar, one of our four, had a relative who owned a plot of land, which was more of an allotment, at a site near Collier Row, adjacent to Romford in Essex. This relative had offered to let us use the allotment and the large garden shed on the grounds that he no longer had any further use for it.

I can still remember the enormous excitement this offer created. Firstly, it was decided to go down to the site on Saturday afternoon, as all of us worked on Saturday mornings. As we intended to stay in the hut on the Saturday night, we each had to provide two blankets etc.

When Friday evening came around we all made our arrangements to transport our equipment, and the place and time of departure. I went to work the following day, Saturday, finishing at about midday. I arrived home, had my lunch and awaited my three companions.

The eldest, 'Bunter' Tibbles, was some two years older than the rest of us. He lived in Pulteney Street, as did George Storrar, whose relative owned the site. George worked in Liverpool Road for Crabb and Co., who manufactured accordions and concertinas. Bobby Reardon worked as an electrician and lived in Thornhill Square. Including me, we became known as the 'Four Maniacs' because of the crazy stunts we got up to on our bikes.

As planned, the other three turned up at my house, 15 College Cross, at just after 14.00 hours in the afternoon. My mother had baked us a large home-made cake and with this in the saddlebag of my bike, we set off to the good wishes of my mother's usual words of wisdom, 'Take care, and don't stay up too late'.

Heading into Park Street, into Canonbury, passed the pub The Canonbury Tavern, across Mare Street, Hackney, through all the back streets until we reached Leytonstone, and passed the

Green Man public house, until we reached Wanstead. Stopping for a drink of water at the fountain opposite the George public house, we carried on down Eastern Avenue until Gants Hill, over the humped-back bridge at Newbury Park until we came to a roundabout, where the sign said, right for Romford and left into Whalebone Lane, then onto Colliers Row. We then had to turn into a road where new houses were still being built and at the end was a slight incline leading up to the allotment.

All the allotments were on ground that had originally formed part of a large manor house which had been burned down some time previously. It was a large site where our allotment was, and the hut was also very big with a large wooden water butt, full of water from the gutters that ran round the hut.

Opening the door of the hut, we found that at the far end was an old Kitchener stove, still in working order, plus some saucepans and other kitchen utensils, a kettle, teapot and buckets.

The stove quickly lit and fuelled with the abundant supply of wood, we proceeded to unload the bikes and took on various tasks. I went down to one of the new houses and obtained a bucket of drinking water, while the others chopped wood and cleared away some of the cobwebs inside the hut. Pooling our resources, we each contributed two shillings, giving us a total of eight shillings for groceries etc. Returning to the corner shop at Colliers Row, we made our purchases of potatoes, sausages, bread, fats, milk, etc., and we all bought a packet of Kensitas.

Once again installed in our hut it befell to me to take charge of the cooking etc. With the flat top of the stove, the kettle was soon boiling along with the sausages spitting in the frying pan and the potatoes cooking. The heat from the stove soon warmed the hut and as it was now approaching dusk; two paraffin oil lamps gave us adequate light.

Quite soon the meal was ready and we all tucked in with great relish, demolishing the first course followed by Lyons' individual apple pies with mugs of steaming hot tea. Time sped quickly by and we began to make up our individual beds, being instructed by 'Bunter' to fold the two blankets longways and use some long safety pins to secure the sides. All of these preparations were carried out with a great deal of laughter and noise. Bobby Reardon had brought along his crystal set wireless and proceeded to operate the 'Cat's Whiskers' and, to our surprise, found by listening on the earphones, that we had picked up the radio signal of the BBC broadcast from a Mayfair hotel in the centre of London. We soon discovered it was a dance orchestra, conducted by the, then famous Harry Roy and his band. Eventually, after a great deal of hilarity lasting until the early hours of Sunday morning, silence reigned.

The following morning was bright and sunny, and someone suggested that we should all immerse ourselves completely in the rainwater butt outside. On stripping off, I jumped into the butt, which not only took my breath away but numbed my whole body – thirty seconds was enough. However, once I had climbed out of the bath and rubbed myself furiously with a towel, I felt my body glowing all over. It was quite a remarkable experience but that was the only time I had the courage to take an early morning dip.

We spent the whole day tending the allotment. I cooked lunch and at about 16.00 hours we locked up the hut and made tracks towards home.

Many times, 'Bunter', George, Rob and I spent the following weekends at the allotment. Each one holds a special memory of times that were happy and reasonably carefree in the beginning of the summer of 1939.

I was now fifteen years of age and basically, like many youngsters of my age, lived for today – tomorrow was long way off. We still met the girls at the bottom of Richmond Road, went to the cinema on Friday evenings, had our bags of chips most nights, talked of staying for a week's holiday at the allotment, little realising or even caring about what was going on in Europe.

One evening I was walking along Matilda Street when I ran into a boy who was friends with me at St Thomas's. Although a little younger than me, he was due to leave school in the August of 1939. Unfortunately for him, he obviously couldn't run as fast as me because on one of his forays into Woolworths in Chapel Street, intent on pinching something, he had been arrested for stealing.

Two weeks later, he had gone before the Care Committee for the purpose of arranging some form of employment when he left school, and this unfortunate episode and his arrest were presented at his interview with members of the Committee. I could tell by his manner that he feared the worst, possibly being sent, like so many other boys from the district, who had been caught stealing, to Borstal. However, a few weeks later I heard that he had appeared in court and had been placed on probation. I recall some of the local boys said at the time, 'Lucky old Eric Goodwin'.

When, in September 1940, the 'Blitz' began Islington, along with many other parts of London, was the target for the German bombers. Eric Goodwin was, with his entire family – parents, brothers and sisters – sheltering in the basement of their house at the top end of Barnsbury Road, near Copenhagen Street. Their house was completely demolished by a direct hit from four bombs, dropped by a German plane. An air raid warden was quoted as saying, at the time of the incident, 'There's a whole family under that lot if the bomb blast hasn't killed them. The water main has burst and the gas mains are alight'.

Needless to say, there were no survivors. Poor old 'Lucky' Eric Goodwin.

A nice open area of grass and children's play area are sited where his and other houses once stood – a simple epitaph to a good friend who knew nothing of war. He only wanted to live and enjoy the only life he knew in Islington.

On Saturday, 2 September 1939, for some reason I was on my own, my three companions being otherwise occupied. However, after lunch I decided to ride down to the allotment on my own and stay the night, returning home on Sunday. I travelled along the usual route until I reached the roundabout at Whalebone Lane, where I stopped for a rest. As I stood by the side of the road, watching the traffic passing to and from London, for some inexplicable reason, I decided there and then, not to go on to the allotment that weekend and I returned home along the same route I had taken earlier. The years have passed and I have never been able to understand why I changed my mind at that particular point in my journey on that particular day.

I reached home and I told my mother I changed my plans about staying over the weekend and went out to meet up with our little gang in Matilda Street. Although there was a fair number of people on the streets around the Caley that night, it somehow seemed a subdued evening by normal Saturday night standards. Eventually, because few of our crowd were around, I felt somewhat bored and returned home to 15 College Cross.

I recall the next day, Sunday, 3 September 1939, very vividly. Most people stayed at home, awaiting the broadcast from the BBC, by the prime minister at that time, Mr Neville Chamberlain. When he eventually spoke on the radio and made the dramatic statement that we, Great Britain, must now accept that a state of war existed between us and Germany, I remember my father sat down, rolled himself a cigarette and said, 'Two bloody lunatics want to rule the world, Hitler and Mussolini.'

Shortly after the broadcast the air raid sirens began the first of many horrible, frightening and wailing sounds, which were to become part of everyday life throughout London and the country for almost the next six years, to give a warning of German air attack.

As the sirens wailed, some people rushed from their homes into the street, pulling on gas masks, which had been issued to each person some months previously, while other people already walking out in the street and some riding bicycles, started to run and pedal their bikes furiously as they made their way home. Panic was very evident and some hysteria because a great may older people imagined that the German bombers were already overhead. After short time the sirens sounded the very welcome "all clear' signal and people began to return to some kind of normality.

On the following morning, Monday, I rode to work in Moorgate and every conversation hinged around the outbreak of war. Outside newspaper stands in the city placards announced the mobilization of the Territorial Army and the Reserves. and talked of the compulsory call-up of men from the age of eighteen years upwards. Plans were being made to evacuate school children in the London area to homes and schools out in the various towns of the English countryside.

Within a week my father decided to leave Islington and stay at Shoeburyness, and I had no alternative but to go with my parents. That ended my employment with the firm of Rotary watches.

After two weeks, we all returned to College Cross and I sought and secured a position with the British Drug Houses in City Road. My only brother at home decided to get married and a few weeks later my father decided to move into a flat in the block of buildings at the top end of Thornhill Road. My eldest brother, already married, was also living in the same block so that this move helped to cheer up my mother who had only me at home to worry about.

The move made little difference to me except that I had a few flights of stairs to climb when I returned home each evening. I still continued to see my grandmother, on my mother's side, who was still living at 26 Lonsdale Square, but she was not keen to walk the extra distance to visit us as she was now over eighty years of age.

My work at the British Drug Houses was as a writer, which kept me inside most of the time, except when I was asked to travel to another part of the firm situated on the other side of the canal which separated the two factories and offices.

To make this hazardous journey, I had to use a contraption, more like a wooden box, which, supported on pulleys, was held aloft by a steel cable. The actual journey across the canal only took about two minutes and I loved using this archaic form of transport and I enjoyed the work.

I still met the gang at Richmond Road and although a lot of older school friends were joining the respective services and coming home in uniform, life carried on much the same as before.

It was around this time that I became associated with an Italian family, named Casalis. There were several brothers and sisters. The youngest son, called Orlando, was some two years older than me and we became friends. He was working as a young hairdresser with his older brother who has a hairdressing shop in the Caledonian Road. The family lived in a house at the bottom end of Copenhagen Street, almost next door to the Milford Haven public house.

Most evenings, Orlando and I would meet either at his house or at the bottom end of Richmond Road. It was on one of our meetings that he introduced me to another Italian family in which there were two sons, one called Gus and the other Bruno.

When the Government introduced a law that all 'aliens' had to register with the police, Bruno and his father duly reported to their local police station. It was at this time that I discovered that Bruno and his father were both born in Italy and were subsequently interned under the 'aliens' law. Gus, the older son, was however, born in England, as was his mother and therefore continued to live in their home in a road leading off from the Caledonian Road. As time progressed, both Bruno and his father, along with several hundred other interned Italians, were to be transported to Canada for the duration of the war. The ship they sailed in was called the *Andorra Star*.

As fate would have it, this ship was torpedoed by a German submarine, in the Atlantic en route to Canada and most of the internees drowned, among them Bruno and his father. This tragic event was followed by a more ironic twist of fate as shortly after being notified by the authorities of the loss of his brother and father, Gus received his call-up papers to join the British Army. I never really understood how Gus felt at this time although he did become a member of the British Army. When the Blitz began I saw Gus couple of times when he was on leave but in due course I lost contact with him and Orlando. On reflection I can only hope that Gus made it through the war.

It was a harsh winter and I got wet many times travelling by bike to and from work. I still went to the pictures on Friday nights and an apathy seemed to fall over people.

The Army and the Air Force were in France, and we heard various war reports on the radio and in the newspapers. Christmas arrived and a lot of snow with it and during the New Year of 1940, Vera Lynn made her record *The White Cliffs of Dover* which one heard endlessly.

Early in the spring my father again decided to move. My poor mother! I had a lot of sympathy for her. This time it wasn't very far away, just round the corner into Westbourne Road to a basement flat.

People were carrying on more or less as normal and everybody was talking about it being a phoney war, although we had some losses in France and at sea. The boys and I even made a couple of visits to the allotments and stayed over the weekends. With the coming of May, things began to accelerate in France, followed at the end of May by the attempted evacuation of our army from Dunkirk. Many soldiers were saved but many were taken prisoner by the Germans. It was very bad time for many families, not only in Islington, but throughout the country, as fathers, brother and sons were reported missing, following the mass evacuation of our troops from Dunkirk. Depression set in and many members of local families could be seen wearing black or black armbands, mourning relatives killed in France.

One sad tale that ended in happiness befell a boy older than me, his name was George Brock, who lived on the street behind St Thomas's, Shirley Street, which no longer exists. George was our school football team goalkeeper and played in the team many times before he left school and started work. In 1940 he was in the Army and in France. Following the evacuation from Dunkirk he was reported as being killed in action. His family went into mourning as did a great many of his school friends.

Some six months or so elapsed, when one day George Brock appeared at the door of his home in Shirley Street, completely unscathed. His mother collapsed with the shock of seeing George alive and well. The loss of so many of our soldiers, airmen and sailors created a depressive state of mind throughout the country, and many young men in Islington volunteered for military service rather than waiting to be called up.

Fears of an invasion by German forces were very much in peoples' minds, now that the French and Belgium governments had capitulated to the Germans, who had marched into the capital of France and were installing themselves in Paris.

Air attacks increased on British airfields situated on the south and east coasts, including airfields on the outskirts of London. Although I was still meeting the gang in Matilda

Street it became very obvious to us all that our nightly get together would soon end.

In Thornhill Square, the RAF had taken over the green park in the centre of the square, installing a barrage balloon which was held down by steel cables when on the ground and winched upwards when German planes crossed our coastline. Everything was put on a true wartime footing, with blackouts, air raid wardens, etc. Cars and lorries had to be fitted with masks over their headlamps with only small slits to allow a filter of light through to illuminate the road. Many people in Islington, not used to streets without lights, sported black eyes and bruises to their heads and bodies where they had walked into lampposts, trees on the pavements and Belisha beacons at pedestrian crossings.

Because the German fighters and bombers could not overcome the RAF during their daytime raids, they switched their bombing raids to endless nighttime attacks on London and other major cities throughout Great Britain. London and the Midlands bore the brunt of the horrific night attacks with not only bombs, but land mines and the horrendous incendiary bombs which exploded on impact, their phosphorus contents burning furiously, setting on fire anything with which they came into contact, particularly houses, shops, office buildings and warehouses.

Because of the increasing number of night raids and the never-ending fires caused by the incendiaries, taxi cabs were commandeered to be used by the Fire Service and the newly formed Auxiliary Fire Service (AFS) for the towing of auxiliary pumps to help quell the fires.

Many families in the heavily bombed districts like Islington, took to finding safety in the Underground stations, taking their children, personal belongings, and previously cooked food to be eaten later. The husbands joined them on the station platforms as they finished work. Before the last trains had ceased running, makeshift beds were laid out on the platform and meals eaten. On several occasions, later on, when I was returning to London on leave from the RAF, I had to tread carefully as I left an Underground train, having reached my destination at King's Cross or Caledonian Road Underground Station because of the mass of peopled and children bedded down on the platforms. On one night whilst on leave, I was traveling to the West End and alighted at the Leicester Square Station and found the platform packed with people sleeping everywhere and I had great difficulty leaving the station as people were laid on every stair of the escalators leading up to street level.

It was an unhappy sight, but the fear of the German bombers drove people to seek safety in the nearest Underground stations. Many people, leaving the station platforms after a night's sleep, returned to a home they had vacated the night before to find it completely demolished; 'bombed out' became the phrase of the day to explain people trying to find further accommodation.

Many times I was an unwilling witness to a scene of householders digging among the ruins of their homes, hoping to find and retrieve items of furniture or personal belongings which were buried when the house was bombed the night before. Even the 'Ginger' tomcat or 'Spot' the dog were sought with great urgency and if fortunate to be found, the reunion often brought a tear to the eye of the sternest official on duty.

Such were some of the scenes in 1940 that are still vivid in my memory of the German bombing.

It was on the evening of 7 September 1940, that an air raid began that was to have an effect on my life that I never anticipated. I was to remember that particular day in September, some four years later on, at an airfield in Belgium.

The afternoon had seen many air raids by the German planes which seemed to ease as the evening begin. Sometime around 20.00 hours, the sirens began to wail their mournful sound and shortly after that one of the heaviest raids by enemy planes began. They concentrated their attack with bombs and incendiaries on the East End of London, quickly setting alight the warehouses and private homes in the area.

The noise of the bombing and of the German planes forced my parents and me out of our home into the road outside. The picture I saw I have never forgotten. German bombers, shinning silver as they were caught in the criss-crossed beams of the British searchlights, while anti-aircraft guns blazed away at them, set against a back cloth of the night sky ablaze with the orange and yellow flames coming from the property set light by the bombs in the East End. It was so bright from the light of the flames that I was easily able to read a copy of the *Daily Express*, I had in my hand. Several bombs were being dropped round us and for safety we returned to the inside of our home. The raid continued throughout the night until, with the break of dawn, the 'all clear' sounded.

As the night clouds moved away, the extent of the damage was very visible, not only in Islington but in every district around and down to the East End of London. I didn't go to work the following day, neither did my mother, as we didn't know if we had a firm to go back to. It was circumstantial that my brothers and their wives, and my sister and her husband decided to call at our home that day. I think that everyone was just checking on each other after the previous night's attack.

The following few days and nights continued with German serial bombardment and few people had any sleep on these terrible nights, in fact most people began to dread the light fading which was a prelude to the beginning of another night of death and destruction. At work the continuous interruptions of air raids during the day caused a series of hold ups as all the staff had to leave whatever job they were doing and take cover in the nearby air raid shelters.

On the Saturday I had met some of the boys and we were walking along Upper Street, just before it joins the bottom end of Liverpool Road, by Chapel Street Market, when the air raid siren was sounded. Although a little apprehensive, we all stood on the high pavement because it was a bright and sunny afternoon, and we could see the British and German fighter planes overhead. So high up were they that you could see the dogfights going on by the twisting and turning of their exhaust vapour trails. It became even more realistic when empty cartridge cases ejected from the planes' machine guns and clattered on to the roof tops of houses and buildings, and bounced into Upper Street. At first we thought it was shrapnel from the anti-aircraft guns but then there was a rush to collect the spent cases as souvenirs, once we realised what the noise was. It was noticeable that cinemas, restaurants and theatres began to close early in the evening and with the winter nights drawing in, the streets looked quite deserted as soon as it got dark.

As the occasion arose I saw some of the old gang at the corner of Matilda Street and Richmond Road by the surgery of old Dr Christy, but gradually we all seemed to be preoccupied with staying close to our home and our meetings became less frequent.

I kept in touch with Olive by calling at her house at 25 Matilda Street and her mother became a very good friend to me then and during the rest of the war. Perhaps because I felt I was now grown up, I tended to spend a lot more time on my own than I had previously. When the opportunity arose and the daytime air raids allowed, I took the time to look at Islington which was experiencing air raids for the second time in just over twenty years, and I recalled the stories my mother had told me concerning the Zeppelin air raids during the First World War. This included the Zeppelin which was shot down, crashing near Cuffley in Hertfordshire, killing over forty German airmen on board. All were buried at Cuffley cemetery.

Similar stories were being told of German planes being attacked by British fighters and shot down in the present war. If the luckless pilot survived the crash or parachuted to safety, woe betide him if he landed in a street in one of the heavily bombed districts in and around London. If the police or soldiers could not get to him first, he or his crew members would receive a very rough time from the local wives and mothers, before being rescued by the military authorities.

Funerals were still being conducted daily around Islington and families being bereaved not only by the bombing but by natural causes. The fact many were still requesting horse-drawn hearses and carriages for the mourners, meant that my father was very busy but as he realised and later confided to me, the writing was on the wall for the use of horse-drawn vehicles.

It is one thing to attend a funeral with horse-drawn transportation but a completely different situation when an air raid began. While the passengers can alight and take shelter, from my father's point of view, he had to remain with the horses. In the event of a bomb dropping too close, the animals would become frightened and bolt in any direction, thus causing an accident or serious injury to themselves. My father's words were prophetic for gradually motor vehicles took over from horses and after the war it was extremely rare to see a funeral with horses being used.

As I have already mentioned, Barnsbury Road (my birthplace) and many adjoining streets suffered extensively from the bombs and land mines that were obviously intended by the German bomb aimers to hit King's Cross, St Pancras or Euston railway stations and unfortunately missed and fell short, destroying one side of Barnsbury Road, Pulteney Street and Gainsford Street etc., leaving a fairly large area of debris and loss of life to young and old alike.

My associations with Islington have been punctuated over the years since the war ended but my recollections of certain events that happened when I was a boy there are still very clear.

It was sometime in 1943 when I was on leave from the RAF that I happened to stop at a coffee/tea stall which was pitched outside the Barnsbury gardens at the junction of Bansbury Road and Richmond Road. It was rare to see such a stall but, nevertheless, inviting at 21.00 hours on a dark evening. It was lit inside by just several candles and the proprietor poured out the tea or coffee into very well used mugs in the gloom of the evening and the wavering candlelight. Hardly romantic, as there was, I recall, a strong smell of candle grease which seemed to taint the flavour of the liquid in the mug. I was alone at the time when I was joined at the stall by a young man and his girlfriend. Because of the gloom surrounding us, I did not recognise the man however, after a moment or two, he called me by my school nickname 'Whiggie' and I realise we were at St Thomas's school together.

The story that he related to me that evening was not only fascinating, but horrendous, bearing in mind that it had happened many hundreds of miles from his home in Islington. Apparently, he had joined the Merchant Navy in 1941 or 1942 and had made many journeys across the Atlantic on convoy duties, ferrying war materials, essential foodstuffs etc. However, on one of his trips with a large convoy of ships across the Atlantic, a number of U-boats – a 'Wolf Pack' – made several night attacks and succeeded in sinking many of the ships, including oil tankers.

The ship this lad was on was one of those sunk by the German torpedoes and he found himself in the sea which was already polluted with oil from the sunken oil tankers. It was several hours before he was rescued by another ship in the convoy. Hardly had he changed into dry clothes and was trying to collect his senses before there was an explosion on the ship which had rescued him. Again, a torpedo sank the ship under his feet and back into the Atlantic he was thrown once more. In all, this boy from the same school as me, spent forty hours in the water, having seen the two ships, his own and his rescuer's sink beneath him. Still suffering from the effects of swallowing mouthfuls of crude oil, he was on leave from the Merchant Navy.

I asked him what he intended doing once his leave ended. 'Go back to sea,' was his prompt reply. I believe his name was Erlicher. I never saw him again.

He too, was another product of Islington. To me, he was an unsung hero. This was another episode during the war I will always remember.

There have been many occasions when I have been in Islington over the years, walking along Upper Street and I have paused at Islington Green where my mother was born to look at the site where the Collins' Music Hall once stood. Long since demolished, it always fascinated me as a young boy. Many times I heard my father describe to me the nights when he was employed to take the performers from one music hall to the next in a Hansom cab. Long before Charlie Chapin became famous in America, my father would transport him and others from an act called Fred Karno's Gang to various halls situated in Shoreditch, Holborn, Holloway and Finsbury Park. These artists were often engaged to perform at perhaps five or six halls during one night and, as time was of the essence, once the artist had finished their act, they would, complete with make-up etc., still on, jump into my father's waiting cab to be driven as fast as the horse could go to the next hall on the list. The procedure was repeated each time until completing the final act of the evening. All this took place just after the turn of the century, in the 1900s. I felt it was a great loss to Islington when the Collins' Music Hall closed for the last time and was knocked down. It had seen two world wars and many of the acts that performed there over the years, went on to become famous stars in the world of entertainment.

Chapel Street, with its every day market, became a Mecca for hundreds of people when I was a small boy and also long before I was born. I have often been able to look upon old photographs of the market taken many years before my first visit with my mother. They always showed Chapel Street packed with shoppers on any day of the week. Many of the well-known names of the stallholders and shopkeepers have long since gone, but there are still great-grandchildren of the original stallholders who continue to carry on the traditions which began so long ago.

Near the White Conduit Street end of the market was the cardboard box factory where dozens of young girls began their first employment after leaving school. Next door was Butler's, a fish shop for many years, which never seemed to close. Then the pub on the corner, the Duke of Denmark, Cloudesley Road with its Victorian dwellings and the tenements in Stonehill Street.

Looking back at the events that happened before the Second World War can be tinged with sadness and nostalgia while others were extremely hilarious. Like the time when, as a small boy with a couple of pals, we ventured down to King's Cross and into Russell Square. Standing on the railings outside a well-known hotel, we watched as the guests sat at tables enjoying their evening meal while a small string orchestra played harmonious background music. I don't know how long I watched this scene, but I remember very clearly, saying to my pals, 'When I grow up I'm going to come here to have my dinner'. Having spent many years travelling extensively, all over the country, staying in excellent hotels, when I was in Russell Square after the war, I was very disillusioned when I entered the same hotel that as a boy I held in such high esteem. I was appalled to see the condition of the dining room. I never did have dinner in that hotel.

At the end of 1940 my father again decided we would move. On this occasion, because of my mother's health and the bombing, he made for a small market town in Buckinghamshire, some 30 miles west of London. Although I had no choice but to go with him, I never really settled in the town and went back after a few months to Islington, staying often with Olive's parents or with my older married brother, visiting my parents at weekends.

I had again to find a new employment and was fortunate to secure a job with a shipping firm with a head office in Northdown Street near King's Cross.

I was now seventeen years of age and many of my friends from school were already in the various armed services. 'Bunter' Tibbles from Pulteney Street was in the RAF, George Storror and Bobby Reardon I lost contact with as I did with some of the girls who made up our little gang, who met at the bottom of Richmond Road.

With my new job, I began to work at a branch office situated at North Road, a turning on the left after the Caledonian Road Underground Station. There were only four office staff at the branch, a senior older man, Mr Smith, another lad the same age as me called John, and a woman telephonist, plus me.

The work was very interesting, and John and I became quite close friends. Often, we would spend the evening together, perhaps visiting the cinema, for instance. The senior man at our office received his Army call-up and left the firm. Shortly after this the telephonist left the company, just leaving John and me to run the branch office. Daytime air raids were less frequent than previously and towards the end of 1941 John and I discussed whether we should wait to be called up for military service or volunteer before then. It transpired that John joined the Army while I volunteered for the RAF.

It was shortly after this decision that I told my parents I had volunteered, not realising the effect it would have on them both. My mother was very apprehensive, but it was my father who I knew as a very strong man and a hard but fair person, that seemed shattered by my announcement that I was joining the RAF. Perhaps because I was so young, he felt I should wait until I was officially called up but, for the first time in my life, I saw him as a very caring father and although he tried hard to conceal his fears for my safety, he was also very proud of my decision.

As it turned out, although only one of my brothers was in the Army and he was invalided out after a year or so, I spent over five years in the RAF, including going for the first time in my life, to Europe during the Normandy landing in France in 1944. During this period, when I was on leave, after visiting my parents in the country, I would invariably spend five or six days back in Islington, returning only on the last day, to spend time with my parents before returning to my squadron.

I can recall one occasion in March 1945, travelling on leave, many hundreds of miles by train and ship from my airfield in Germany and eventually arriving early in the morning at Victoria Station, going on the Underground to King's Cross and walking from the station towards Pentonville Road, past the well-known jewellers shop Bravingtons, turning left into the Caledonian Road and continuing along to turn into Copenhagen Street, up past my old school St Thomas's in Everilda Street, into Richmond Road and stopping outside my birthplace at 162 Barnsbury Road.

I don't remember how long I stood outside my previous home but looking around at the bomb damage at the top end of the road, and recalling the very extensive damage and destruction I had helped to bring about in Germany, had a two-fold effect on me at the time.

Firstly, I felt justified about the havoc that the RAF had caused in Germany, particularly when I recalled the many school friends and their families who were killed in the nighttime air raids by the German bombers in my part of Islington in 1940 and onwards. At the same time, recalling the fear I felt when I was on the ground, on the receiving end on the nights in 1940, unable to hit back at the German bombers.

The second thought being saddened by the damage I saw in Pulteney Street and the surrounding area and the obvious fact that so many people I had known over the years no longer lived in the houses in the many streets I grew up in.

I eventually walked into Chapel Street Market and sat in one of the cafes, drinking a cup of tea, looking into space, while by mind tried to take in all that had happened to me between

This portrait of Ron Chapman was taken in 1941 at Bertolle's studio, which was located at the junction of Richmond Road and (The Caley) Caledonian Road in London. Ron was 17 years of age with a 19-inch waist at the time.

René Mouchotte's pin, which was given to Ron Chapman by Madame Mouchotte.

Ron Chapman's FAFL badge, which he always wore with his blazer.

Above left: Ron Chapman pictured in September 1944. This portrait was taken at 36, Rue de Lille, Menen.

Above right: Ron's dear friend Andre Debael, pictured at Menin in Belgium.

Drope airfield near Lingen, Germany, on 26 April 1945 – Ron's 21st birthday. With the ground crew of 345 (GC II/2 'Berry') Squadron.

Right: Three Armourers pictured at Fairword Common near Swansea, February 1945. From left to right are The Duke, Tomo and Griff.

Below: The late Wee Jock Crawford of 340 (Île-de-France) Squadron.

Left: Corporal George Blaikie of No.341 (Alsace) Squadron at Antwerp, Belgium.

Below: Groundcrew of No.485 (New Zealand) Squadron at Maldegem, Belgium.

Groundcrew of No.485 (New Zealand) Squadron at Maldegem, Belgium.

Another view of personnel of No.485 (New Zealand) Squadron at Maldegem, Belgium.

Pictured at Fassberg, Germany, are, from left to right, Bob, Ron, Griff and The Duke.

Ken Griffiths' and Gladys' wedding day in March 1946. Ron Chapman was the best man. Also present is Ken's sister.

Above: Ron Chapman standing on the runway at Wevelgem airstrip in Belgium, 1980.

Right: Ron Chapman at Brookwood Cemetery on Sunday, 31 May 1992.

Ron Chapmen among the Free French graves at Brookwood Cemetery on Sunday, 31 May 1992.

Ron's sons, Mark and Nigel Chapman, at Brookwood in 1992.

September 1940 when I first saw the London sky red with flame and now, in March 1945. I found it extremely difficult to fully understand how I had changed, not only in years, but as a result of the carnage I, like so many others, had witnessed, not only in Great Britain but also in Europe.

I returned a week later to Germany and the war. The death and destruction continued but my feelings never changed as I began to realise that in any situation war not only destroys cities but human bodies and minds.

Chapter 5

2nd Tactical Air Force

It was on 10 September, that I presented myself to the recruiting centre near Euston Station and along with many other young men we travelled from Paddington Station to a deserted school in Penarth, just outside Cardiff, Wales. Here we were all billeted in the local civilian houses, the owners having been evacuated some time before. The conditions were austere to say the least, however, after five days our entire group travelled onto Weston-super-Mare where we spent some six weeks square bashing and then I was transferred to RAF Credenhill near Hereford. I remained at Credenhill for six months undergoing training with many others on the maintenance and use of all types of guns and armaments involved with RAF fighters and bombers. Early the following March, I received seven days' leave and a posting to No. 2 Air Gunnery School situated at Dalcross, some 9 miles from Inverness, Scotland.

For a lad born in London my first experience of Scotland was quite enlightening, I think the furthest I had travelled in my life was possibly a 50 mile radius of London. Therefore the vastness of Scotland was difficult to take in, although I found the Scottish people very hospitable and generous.

At the air gunnery school approximately every six weeks, groups of sixty potential air gunners were trained in all aspects of air gunnery. After this period, there was a passing out parade when the men who had passed the course were presented with their sergeants' stripes and the air gunner's brevet.

After the ceremony the men were sent on seven days' leave and a week or so following this, they found themselves aboard an operational British bomber, as front, upper or rear gunners en route to Occupied Europe. Of the many who passed their air gunnery course at Dalcross, it was only a matter of weeks before a red ring drawn in ink surrounding an air gunner's face on a group photograph fixed to the CO's office wall, made one realize that the air gunner was either missing or dead.

With some groups who had passed their course it would often be only a month before the whole group photograph was completely covered in red circles. Such was the destruction of air crews during the Second World War. I enjoyed the beauty of Scotland and in particular Inverness and as I was doing some flying on training flights, places like Banff, Elgin, the Moray Firth were a pleasure to see from the air. It was about the end of 1943, that I noticed an influx of different regiments at Fort George, situated some 3 miles away from Dalcross. There were nightly exercises with tanks and assault craft, very soon it became obvious to us all on the station that the Second Front was not too far away.

Life at RAF Dalcross carried on as normal, flying most days when weather permitted. An opportunity to volunteer for the Fleet Air Arm came along but although I put my name down along with two friends, I never heard of anymore.

It was on 14 May 1944 that the Orderly Room at No. 2 Air Gunnery School at Dalcross, received a signal to post three armourers to No. 485 'New Zealand' Squadron of the 2nd Tactical Air Force, stationed at Church Norton, Selsey, near Chichester. Circumstances prevailed that I was one of the three armourers selected to travel south and within twenty-four hours, the three of us had journeyed from Inverness and found ourselves on a Spitfire Operational Squadron at Selsey, on the 15 May 1944. At the time I thought how strange it was that the powers that be at headquarters should send me from one end of the country to the other.

Up until this time my service life had been fairly orderly in the RAF, however, after travelling for a day and a half by train from Inverness to Chichester in Sussex, my first day on an operational Spitfire squadron soon shook the complacency out of me.

I arrived at Chichester about 20.30 hours in the evening after travelling overnight by train from Inverness. To find the crew chief, I was advised to look for him in the Globe Public House, next to the railway station. When at last I was able to locate him, he told me I would have to wait until the pub closed before I could get a lift to the squadron at Selsey (Church Norton) some 8 miles away.

At closing time, the Crew Chief staggered out of the Globe Public House and told me to climb into the adjacent truck parked outside. After lurching along the dark country lanes, I arrived with a great deal of trepidation at the tented section of No. 485 (New Zealand) Squadron. By this time, it was now completely dark, and I could not take in the size of the area, however, I was given two musty blankets and shown a tent.

Inside with the help of a torch I discovered two other occupants already asleep and making the best of it I made a makeshift bed. I don't think I will ever forget that first night at Selsey, as I felt I was sleeping on a ploughed field, but eventually I managed to fall asleep.

At 05.00 hours in the morning, not my best time to be awakened, the noise from outside the tent was deafening and, staggering to my feet, I poked my head outside, to be met by blinding sunlight and this awful noise. All around me were Spitfires being revved up and made ready for take-off. The noise was devastating and indeed it was some time before I understood the early morning activity which was part of a fighter squadrons existence. Nevertheless, the sound of the engine of a Spitfire taking off is indeed unique – once heard, never forgotten.

While I had been stationed in Scotland, I enjoyed reasonable billets with normal toilet facilities, here at Church Norton on 485 Squadron everyone was under canvas as were the rest of the 2nd TAF. As for toilet facilities they were non-existent except for open buckets, with a few yards of canvas as an attempt to give the occupants a little privacy and the open sky as a roof and at the mercy of the elements.

Life in 485 Squadron was very hectic, the ground crews were on the go from dawn until dusk. The life was tough, dirty, and very tiring with very little opportunity to keep oneself clean.

Meals were a non-star, open air variety, when it wasn't the food, it was defending what resembled food half cooked or cold, from swarms of the largest wasps I have ever seen, plus the dust and the dirt for an aperitif, such was my introduction to operations in 1944.

The fact that squadrons within the 2nd TAF were completely mobile and therefore all accommodation was tented, gave us newcomers a sharp education into the day-to-day existence of living and working, rain or shine, out in the elements in the Sussex countryside. After the comfort of the standard billets of the RAF station at Inverness, this open-air style of life soon shook the complacency out of us as we tried to integrate ourselves into the life of the squadron at Selsey.

Over a period of a month, during which time 485 (New Zealand) Squadron moved its base several times from Selsey to Horsham, then Merston, we finally set up camp at Funtingdon, near Chichester.

It would appear that by this time my fame had spread throughout the south coast of England, for in June 1944 I was summoned to the tented orderly room of 485, to be informed that I was posted to 340 'Ile de France' Free French Squadron, part of the No. 145 French wing, based at Selsey. This wing also contained three other French squadrons, Nos. 329, 341 and, later on No. 345. All the air crews on these squadrons were made up of Free French pilots flying Spitfires. The CO of No. 341 was Captain Martel who sadly was killed in January 1945 in Europe. It was being part of No. 341 that I experienced the friendly relationships which developed between the French pilots and the British ground crews. Here again everyone was under canvas and as the squadron was flying continuous sorties, I soon made friends with both pilots and my fellow ground crew.

Having said my 'goodbyes' to my two original companions from Inverness, I cleared 485 Squadron and made travel arrangements to proceed to Selsey immediately.

I have some wonderful memories of my time with 485. The pilots were a grand bunch with a marvellous sense of humour and mostly the same age as me. The 'Kiwis' left a remarkable impression of those brave and gallant young men from far away New Zealand. After the landings at Normandy, 485 Squadron was to join up with the French wing.

Regrettably, by the next time I met up with the squadron in Europe, a number of the pilots who I had known during my time at Selsey and Funtington had been killed.

A popular song of the day, which I heard being played repeatedly at Funtingdon, with 485, was *Long Ago and Far Away*. This haunting melody seemed to be a wonderful epitaph to those New Zealand men from far away, who gave their lives for this country's call to arms.

The former CO of No. 486 'New Zealand' Typhoon Squadron, Group Captain Desmond Scott, wrote to me from his home in New Zealand in 1986, ending his letter with – 'Take care and say a short prayer on behalf of all members of 485 Squadron when next you visit Tangmere.' I believe that extract does in fact say it all.

Having reached Chichester in 1944, I made the normal enquiries, via the Personnel Transit Centre and was directed to a village called Sidlesham, which backed onto the grass runways at Church Norton, Selsey. On arrival at Sidlesham, the Orderly Room was manifest in the shape of a semi-detached house on the main road. I have always remembered this house because on entering, I found that all the interior doors of the property were missing, and the back door had been removed completely. Through the gaping hole I could clearly see the Spitfires, dispersed around Church Norton.

Having established my presence, I was directed across the nearby field to where 340 Squadron was sited. (The house used as the Orderly Room at Sidlesham in 1944, was returned to its pre-war glory after the war had ended and has been named 'Green Woods'. I trust that the interior doors have been replaced.)

On 18 May 1944, 329 Squadron was still at Merston and was visited by General Koenig and General Valin who met the pilots. A week later Air Marshal Coningham visited the airfield.

Two days later, on 27 May 1944, Lieutenant Colonel Fleurquin left for headquarters in London where he attended the ceremony of the presentation of the *Croix de Guerre* to the station commander, Group Captain Malan, and Wing Commander Alan Deere.

Another happy occasion followed when Flight Sergeant Traisnel was married at Hitchin in Hertfordshire on 4 June 1944. Both Captain Marchelidon and Captain Colonieu were at the ceremony to represent 329 Squadron.

While the French Wing was stationed at Merston during the previous month of April, the commander-in-chief of the forthcoming *Overlord* D-Day invasion, General Dwight Eisenhower, chose to spend a few days in the historic town of Chichester. His stay was from Wednesday, 19 April until Saturday, 22 April 1944 at the well-known haunt of the Allied fighter pilots, the Ship Hotel.

This historic hotel, unique in its location and cuisine, was during General Eisenhower's visit, chosen by the RAF at Tangmere as the venue for a dinner to be held in honour of the commander-in-chief.

The evening proved to be very successful and was unknowingly a prelude to the forthcoming invasion of Europe on D-Day. Fortunately, the RAF at Tangmere and the management of the Ship Hotel had the foresight to preserve the entire dinner menu and seating arrangements from that evening in 1944.

The guest list contained over sixty senior ranking officers of the RAF and included not only the British but many Allied air marshals, air vice marshals, group captains, wing commanders and squadron leaders of the 2nd Tactical Air Force. Amongst the Allied officers were representatives from America, Poland, South Africa, Belgium and Free France. Wing Commander de Soomer was from the Belgian squadron and Commandant Bernard Duperier was from the Free French wing.

Although I had visited Chichester many times since the end of the war, I had never taken the opportunity of entering the Ship Hotel until one summer evening in 1986, accompanied by my wife, I was prompted, for some inexplicable reason to enter the lounge bar of the hotel. When we were both seated, I found myself looking at a large reproduction of a dinner menu, framed and hanging on the wall. On closer inspection I discovered to my amazement, that it was a black and white copy of the original dinner menu from the reception given in honour of General Dwight Eisenhower, way back in 1944.

The Ship Hotel, Chichester, is one of a group of hotels under the umbrella of the Mermaid Hotels of Rye in Sussex. This group is owned by Michael K. Gregory. I wrote to this gentleman and he generously allowed me to take a copy of the menu for inclusion in this book and did in fact, take the trouble to show me the original plan which hangs in his personal office at another location. The original was depicted in colour in illuminated style and measured about two feet six inches square.

Sadly, many of the pilots and officers featured are no longer with us and therefore it is a tribute to them that they will be remembered for posterity by this simple action of the staff at the Ship Hotel.

Chapter 6

D-Day

On 5 June 1944, activity was pretty hectic. Numerous sorties were being flown over Caen and the squadron ground crews worked diligently to service and re-arm the Spitfires, right up until darkness drove the light from the sky. D-Day exploded on 6 June 1944, creating a date that will be forever prominent in the annals of history.

The French squadrons were airborne from early light, flying in continuous sweeps over the Normandy beaches. On 7 June, Wing Commander Compton, flying with No. 329 Squadron, attacked a JU 88 as it was making for cloud at three thousand feet over Caen. He fired a five second burst at the enemy aircraft, saw its port wing catch fire, then spiral towards the ground where it crashed.

All three French Squadrons, 329, 340 and 341, moved on 22 June 1944, from Merston to Funtingdon, proceeding to Church Norton near Selsey on 1 July. It was during this month that No. 74 Squadron also joined the French wing making a total of four squadrons on the wing at Selsey.

On 9 July 1944 both 340 and 341 squadrons were ordered on a sweep over Dieppe to escort 200 Lancaster bombers. They were attacked over Rouen by a superior force of Bf 109s. In the dogfight that ensued, Wing Commander Compton and the

CO of 340, Commandant Fournier, each shot down one of the German fighters.

Captain Michel Boudier, attacking another enemy plane, found himself being attacked by a P-47 Thunderbolt fighter. His aircraft began to emit smoke and his Spitfire spiralled downwards. Later on, a parachute was seen in the area. He was reported missing from operations. Captain Boudier was the first pilot to join the squadron with over 275 operational hours and he had taken part in 175 operational sweeps and patrols. He had destroyed seven enemy aircraft, was the holder of the DFC and was a very experienced and likeable pilot.

It was whilst the French wing was stationed at B.85 Schjindel in Holland, at the end of March 1945, that a 341 Squadron ground crew flight rigger, Corporal George Blaikie, heard a voice call out to him: 'Are you still with us Jock?' He discovered it was Captain Boudier who had been in a PoW camp. When the Russians advanced, forcing the Germans to retreat, all the prisoners in the camp were released. Captain Boudier, a very old friend of the late Commandant Mouchotte and Commandant Martel, was on his way back to find his family in France.

On 10 July, Lieutenant Girardon was promoted to command 'B' Flight, replacing Captain Boudier.

At the repair and inspection hangar at Selsey, the French pilots and ground crews celebrated the French National Day (Bastille Day) on 14 July. More excitement was to come two days later, when a member of the ground crew discovered his tent, destroyed by fire.

Commandant Schloesing, *Croix de Guerre*, DFC, was posted back to 340 Squadron at Selsey, early in July. He had been a squadron leader when he was shot down over France on 13 February 1943. Returning to England on 8 May, he spent much of his time in and out of hospital, where he endured seven skin grafting operations as a result of severe burns to his face.

Having established myself with the 340 Squadron at Selsey, I soon found that the work of servicing and maintaining the Spitfires was every bit as hectic as it had been at 485 Squadron. As on most squadrons within the 2nd TAF, there was a good mix of Scots, Welsh, English, Irish and French ground crews.

Two of the first acquaintances I made among the armourers was a lad from Sheffield, Walter (Timber) Wood and a London man, much older than most of us, James Manaton; both very friendly and helpful. It transpired that some five months later they were both killed at an airfield near Antwerp in Belgium. Whenever the occasion has arisen since the war, that I have been in the Chichester area, I have made the pilgrimage along the narrow country lane that leads to the old airfield at Church Norton, Selsey, and remember with clarity, the faces of the two friends, LAC Wood and LAC Manaton. The cold soil of Antwerp in Belgium, in which they are buried is far from the warmth of the Yorkshire Dales and the closeness of the London district where they belonged.

It was during the month of July 1944, late one afternoon, when little flying had taken place, that I heard a sound which I presumed to be a British bomber in trouble and in search of a suitable landing strip. The engine noise became even more extreme, until suddenly, the shape of an aircraft fuselage with clipped wings and flame coming from the rear end, broke through the low cloud over the runway at Church Norton. As quickly as it appeared, it had gone, disappearing in a further bank of low cloud. It vanished from view, still transmitting the echoing engine noise.

I discovered later that it was a V-1 rocket, an example of the terror weapon with which Hitler had threatened to bomb London out of existence. This was but a hint of the fear that I was to experience, when on the receiving end of both the V-1 and V-2 rocket weapons, in the late November and December of 1944, during the six weeks I was in Antwerp in Belgium, when the French wing was based at B.70 Deurne aerodrome.

A few days later when the Selsey weather had improved substantially, I witnessed an American B-17 Flying Fortress crash land near the Flying Control, a private house taken over during the war and in use as the French wing's control tower. The house, named Orchard Cottage, was returned to the owner after the war; it stands on the field and could tell many a tale if only walls could speak.

Several wounded crew members were transported to hospital from the Flying Fortress but a waist air gunner and the rear turret gunner were found dead in their positions in the aircraft.

I was surprised to find that in charge of the repair and inspection section of the French wing at Church Norton was one Alan (Lofty) Knott, a sergeant armourer who had been at Dalcross, when I was based there. He was well liked by the ground crews in general and succeeded in bringing a little humour into a sometimes grim world of reality, where death was always waiting in the wings. Tall and with very dark hair, one could always be sure of catching sight of 'Lofty', either leaving or entering one of the ale houses of which Chichester seemed to have a surfeit. He was always in the company of a few other NCOs on their off-duty excursions.

On 18 July 1944, the four squadrons, comprising forty-eight aircraft of 74, 329, 340 and 341, took off from Church Norton to attack a substantial railway centre in constant use by the Germans for transporting their strategic war materials. Nos. 74 and 329 were led by Commandant J. Fournier in what proved to be a successful sweep.

On 20 July six aircraft of 340, led by Commandant Schloesing, *Croix de la Libération, Croix de Guerre*, DFC, were to escort two Mosquito Pathfinders over St Omer. The Flight involved in a sweep over the target area at 30,000 feet, met very extensive, heavy flak. The following day, 21 July, French pilot Lieutenant Lents, succeeded in crash landing his Spitfire on the airfield at Manston, when his aircraft caught fire at about 600 feet.

A wing escort over Ouistreham, covering a group of Mitchell bombers, encountered heavy flak and two of the Mitchells were seen to explode in mid-air. Sous Lieutenant Lepape experienced engine trouble and was forced to land in France.

Returning to Church Norton after the last sortie of the day on 23 July 1944, the pilots organised an evening for the ground crews at the dispersal. A piano was borrowed from the tented NAAFI plus three barrels of beer and *vin rouge libre* was in evidence. The ground crews had an enjoyable time.

No. 340 Squadron received an intelligence officer and a new pilot, a Czech national, Flight Officer Mazurek. There was a scare when a parachute was seen descending over the airfield at Selsey. After careful inspection it turned out to be a balloon from the Met Office.

Thirty-six aircraft, twelve each from 329, 340 and 341 squadrons, led by Commandant Fournier, *Croix de Guerre*, escorted fifty-four Mitchell bombers en route to bomb St Malo on 1 August 1944. The following day the entire French wing, led by Colonel Fleurquin, *Légion d'honneur, Croix de Guerre*, escorted a hundred Halifax bombers in an attack on German installations near Hazebrouck.

During that period when the French wing was based at Church Norton, the ground crews found that there were cryptic messages left in the wells of the wings on the Spitfires returning from sorties over France. They were from servicing commandos of the 2nd TAF. That particular group of operational crews had been specially organised to service aircraft landing on the front-line airstrips and were extremely close to the battle area in Normandy. The messages that the armourers usually found when they came to re-arm the guns, were requests for a supply of bottles of beer. Considering the terrible heat and dust of the Normandy area, it was not long before a two-way service began. Our pilots collected souvenirs supplied by the servicing commandos in exchange for a supply of beer provided by the Church Norton ground crews. This strictly unofficial service carried on until the French wing eventually landed in Normandy some two weeks later.

On 25 July, General Bouscat visited the three Free French squadrons at Church Norton, accompanied by the AOC, Air Vice Marshal L.O. Brown, General Valin and Air Commodore

Beaumont. In the afternoon the two French squadrons, 340 'Ile de France' and 341 'Alsace', gave a brilliant display of formation flying, concluding with two perfect Crosses of Lorraine emblazoned across the Sussex sky.

Wing Commander Crawford-Compton led thirty-six aircraft from 329, 340 and 341 squadrons on 26 July, to escort a battle group of Mitchells whose target was an extensive fuel dump south of Fontainebleau. The bomb aimers scored some direct hits on the dump although the aircraft encountered very heavy flak. Lieutenant Homolle of 340, reported a glycol leak on his aircraft and went down in France, reported missing in action. Over the Neuborg area, Lieutenants Sanlys and Borndy and Sergeant Chapman were successful in attacking a German flak unit, killing many German personnel. Sergeant Chef Mathey landed in France and the rest of the Squadrons returned to England.

All four squadrons of 145 Wing: 74, 329, 340 and 341 took part in an operation in August 1944 to escort over one hundred Lancaster and Halifax bombers en route to bomb a fuel and ammunition dump at Montrichard. The wing was attacked by a large force of Bf 109s and Fw 190s.

Sous Lieutenant Le-lang was shot down north of Tours, whilst Sergeant Troullet attacked and was successful in shooting down two Bf 109s. Following the dog fight, he landed in France but later returned to England.

The French wing received a signal to move to RAF Tangmere, some 10 miles away. Apart from servicing the Spitfires of the wing and making arrangements to move all the tents and equipment the ground crews had an extremely busy day, beginning with an early morning sortie.

The wing eventually left Selsey for Tangmere in a convoy which took four and a half hours. Although the direct route is only a 10-mile distance, the wing travelled 54 miles (bags of petrol). We were erecting tents and establishing where the various trades and sections were to be based until well after midnight on 6 August 1944.

Rumours of the wing leaving for France were abundant and all leave was cancelled, which did little to calm the nerves. Several members of the ground crews from various trades, took the opportunity to make a last effort to visit their wives and children or parents, by going 'absent without leave'. The motive was not desertion but a need to see loved ones in the apprehension before landing on the shores of Normandy. Ninety-nine per cent of the crews who vanished from the camp at Tangmere did return to their squadrons, albeit they were put on a charge and took their medicine from the commanding officer without complaint.

As a member of the ground crews, I was not alone when I caught a train from Chichester to Victoria and then travelled by various means to my parents' home in Buckinghamshire. How I avoided the dreaded Military Police at Victoria is of no consequence but several unfortunates of both RAF and Army personnel were caught without their obligatory leave pass.

I witnessed one of my own colleagues being apprehended just outside the station. His 'V' for victory sign to me as he was marched away by the Military Police, was typical of the *esprit de corps* that existed between fellow members of the squadron. Regretfully, this man, who never made it home, lost his life during the European campaign, serving No. 340 Squadron when he was killed by enemy action. He was well liked and a wonderful friend to me and others.

A few days after my return to the squadron, I was servicing a Spitfire, when my feet slipped on the metal covering the wings of the aircraft and I crashed onto the concrete runway below, striking the back of my head, where I had had a previous injury. A short trip by ambulance from the sick-bay to the hospital in Chichester ensued. A strong cup of tea was administered by one of the nurses and X-rays were taken. The doctor diagnosed slight concussion; I was still warm so was therefore given a chit for light duties only. I recall with a smile, that our chiefy, Flight Sergeant Feeney, looked at the chit which I had presented with great aplomb and promptly gave me the task of stripping down both 20-millimetre cannons from a Spitfire which had crash landed in one of the furthermost points of Tangmere.

The fact that having removed both cannons from the crashed aircraft, I would have to carry same back to the squadron armoury, was not lost on me or Chiefy Feeney who was still holding my chit for light duties. Needless to say, I never did have the opportunity to enjoy the so-called 'light duties' throughout my service with 340 Squadron.

From Tangmere on 14 August, while the Squadron was patrolling over the Lisieux and Argenton area, Sous Lieutenant Gaudon and Sergeant Chef Cermalacce were reported missing after crashing in France. Taking off again, the squadron of twelve aircraft patrolled the same area, led by Captain Andrieux DFC, to escort bombers in the destruction of operational targets. Adjutant Foissac dived down almost to ground level to investigate activity on the ground and was immediately hit by flak and forced to land in France, minus his flaps.

Another sortie by 329, 340 and 341 Squadrons, led on this occasion by Commandant Christian Martel DFC, on 16 August 1944, to attack the area of Fismes with bombs. On take-off from Tangmere, Sergeant Troullet collided with an aircraft of 340 Squadron and was killed.

The move to France began on 17 August 1944, when half of the Wing's ground crews were moved in the first instance, to a transit area at Old Sarum in Hampshire. When we arrived, I was amazed by the vast quantity of vehicles – trucks, tanks etc. – lined up on every available field and road. Once we entered Old Sarum, security was tight, no one was allowed out of the camp. All the telephones were out of bounds except in the public houses, military police were everywhere.

Somehow some order prevailed although with so many fighter squadrons camped around, I marvelled at the administration. Our squadron ground crews had been split into two groups, one half were once again stationed at Tangmere, whilst the rest of us with most of the trucks and equipment were at Old Sarum. The idea was that once we landed in France, the smaller group at Tangmere would then join us in training. With our half of the ground crews (I was in A Section) we were only at Old Serum a matter of hours and once again we were split into smaller groups of twelve men and given a code number.

This number was relayed over the Tannoy system, we picked up our personal kit and made for the trucks. I recall it was quite dark and about 16.30 hours the convoy of trucks began to move. Travelling away from Old Serum, I found it difficult to establish which direction we were heading for, however, I eventually recognized that we were heading towards the town of Gosport in Hampshire.

It was still dark when we arrived in Gosport and difficult to see what was going on but I could just make out the silhouettes of a fixed number of all types of landing craft. Waiting in the back of the truck, I couldn't imagine how all of us would be able to get onto these small craft.

Eventually everyone jumped down from the trunks and in single file we started to board the landing craft. As each craft filled with men, it started its engine and moved out of the harbour. This procedure carried on, it seemed, for hours until a vast armada of ships and landing craft had formed outside Gosport harbour waiting for darkness to fall again. Gradually the whole group of ships began to move out into the open sea surrounded by an escort of destroyers and motor torpedo boats.

It became very obvious to us all that our large convoy of snipers and escorts was heading in the direction of France, and I noticed a continuous surveillance by the destroyers and torpedo boats that were accompanying us. The fact that the night sky was very dark did little to overcome the feeling of uncertainty and apprehension.

At this time our Free French wing was commanded by Group Captain 'Sailor' Malan and because the ground crews were split into two sections, I found myself aboard this landing craft with some French and British ground crew and not necessarily from my own squadron No. 341 F.A.F.L.

Somehow this convoy of ships made its way towards the French coast. I recall that around 04.00 in the morning suddenly seeing what resembled some small houses set in a massive sandy beach. Never having been to France before, I and many of my fellow ground crew wondered what fate had in store for us. With somewhat of a shudder our landing craft crunched onto the beach, the landing ramp was quickly winched down and everyone moved forward with an urgency which can only be described as fear. We had arrived in Arromanches, Normandy (Gold Beach).

It was only then did I realize the size of this enormous seaborne operation, everywhere one looked there was intense activity. The Beachmasters controlling the flow of trucks and other traffic were busy directing convoys of assorted vehicles which were being discharged from the newly arrived ships.

I have never been able to discover how our ground crews all managed to reach Sommerview airstrip, a short distance from the beach, but somehow all the crews did turn up. Regardless, I was only too pleased to see the sun slowly sink in the sky later that day, as the heat had been unbearable combined with the Normandy sand and the endless numbers of flies and wasps that continually surrounded us.

As normal we had set up our tents on the airstrip and after mounting guards, most of us endeavoured to get some sleep, knowing full well that our Spitfires would be arriving as soon as day broke, somewhere around 04.00 hours the next morning. For some time, I lay awake, listening to the gunfire from the front line just a few miles away, eventually drifting away into a deep sleep.

The following morning I awoke to brilliant sunshine and a clear blue sky. Overhead we could see our Spitfires, three squadrons of them, and as they landed the ground crew ran out to greet them. Very quickly the aircraft were serviced and in a very short time they were airborne again. This operation as repeated some seven more times during the daylight hours until dusk heralded the end of the day's sorties. From a full squadron of twelve aircraft No. 341 by the end of the day had two Spitfires missing, one aircraft crashed killing the pilot, whilst another plane force landed and the pilot was able to walk away from his damaged plane.

After three days in France the residue of ground crews arrived from England, many looking rather bleary red, apparently a vast majority of them had spent their last night in the Brighton pubs before leaving for France, hence their somewhat tawdry appearance.

Now that the French wing had its full complement of ground crews, each of the squadrons allotted itself a separate part of the airstrip for its working and living arrangements. Although the squadron stay comprised the back of a Bedford truck and sleeping accommodation for the areas was tented or anywhere else one could find to sleep. Once organized the inter-squadron rivalry took up where it had left off, the flight mechanics, riggers, instrument bashers, etc., keeping to their own groups of eight to a tent, whilst the armourers, photographers and general duty men were doing likewise with corporals of varying trades being integrated amongst their own ground crews. Although sergeants upwards and officers invariably had tents to themselves.

It was following a few more days at Sommerview that an order was from headquarters was received with the instruction that all personnel should exchange our blue battledress for the Army khaki battledress. As it turned out it was one of the more sensible orders to come from headquarters during the invasion of France for the following reason. It had been established by tragic events that British fighters had shot up British ground troops advancing through France and had mistaken them for German troops in retreat. This incident was caused by the RAF blue uniforms becoming faded in the continuous daily rays of the sun, plus the effect of the Normandy sand. The combination tended to turn our uniforms into the look of the field grey of the German troops.

Once established in Army khaki battledress, I felt safer from attack yet very strange when trying to identify fellow crew members. However, within a week the wing was ordered to move forward as the Allied troops were advancing towards Caen where there had been intense and severe fighting.

Again, the wing split into two sections, the smaller group remaining behind, while the majority of us packed all the equipment into the trucks and left Sommerview about 04.00 hours in the morning heading towards Caen. After some miles of diversions and a very bumpy ride the convoy entered the town of Caen, and one could see the extent of this major battle. The centre and the outskirts of the town being completely destroyed.

Much to my surprise the convoy of our trucks continued onwards, and it was late in the afternoon when we eventually reached the town of Bernay and set up our tents and equipment on the airstrip just outside the town. Within the hour our Spitfires were circling, waiting for instructions to land, having been serviced from the airstrip at Sommerview by the caretaker ground crew left behind. Twenty-four hours later and we were again re-joined by them at Bernay. Our time at the Bernay airstrip was very short but we lost some planes and pilots, which also had a very bad effect on the ground crews of the missing planes.

It was during our stay at Bernay that our squadron lost a pilot in a bizarre accident. Several Spitfires were taking off on their sortie, when one of the last planes was taxiing along the grass runway and as it lifted from the ground a Bedford truck appeared and crossed in front of the path of the Spitfire. In the collision that followed the Spitfire tipped up onto its nose projecting the French pilot out of the cockpit of the plane. It was only when rescuers ran to his aid, that it was discovered that his legs were still in the plane, the impact had torn his body off at the top of his legs.

My first awareness of the lack of food and the extent of malnutrition in France appeared one day on the edge of the airstrip at Bernay. Three young girls walked down a lane towards me and a fellow armourer and asked us for food. I noticed that all three seemed very thin and had sores on their arms and legs. The eldest spoke English and told me she was eighteen and that her two companions were sixteen. At the time I guessed them to be about twelve years of age, such was their condition.

From Bernay we moved as before through to Abbeville, the only outstanding point to retell is that more than two thirds of the ground crews went down with food poisoning and dysentery whilst operating from the airstrip. I have never seen flies so enormous and with the temperature in the mid-eighties it was a wonder that we survived our stay at Abbeville.

After four days we left Abbeville at the unearthly hour of 04.00 hours and I, for one, was not sorry to see the back of this French town. This time our convoy of trucks moved onwards towards Lille, operating from an airstrip quite near Vendeville where the wing spent some five days. Air capacity was pretty hectic and the ground crews worked from around 02.00 hours in the morning until midnight maintaining the Spitfires.

Shortly before leaving Vendeville, Tony Mattick, with 'Wee Jock Cranford', our squadron photographer, and me embarked with a few others on a visit one evening to Lille. For some odd reason our squadron, No. 341, had been stood down enabling the ground crews a short respite. During the course of the evening Tony and I accompanied by two French sisters we had met, found ourselves separated from the main group with the result that we were completely lost and walking in the opposite direction away from Vendeville. It was about 02.00 in the morning when Tony found the end of the tram lines, which we promptly followed back into Lille. Arriving eventually in the centre of Lille, I was surprised to see the two gnomes that had disappeared from the entrance of Kimbells in Chichester, sitting either side of the main doors of the town hall. The next day orders were received for the whole wing to move into Belgium. Little did any of us realise the impact the events in Belgium would have on our lives that followed.

Chapter 7

Menin – Wevelgem

The wing made an early morning move from Vendeville, no one getting any sleep the previous night mainly because of the lateness of the last sortie and the fact that our squadron, No. 341, suffered some casualties – we lost three of our Spitfires with their pilots. It was uncanny the feeling of loss that all the ground crews felt when a plane failed to return and the other crews watched as the crews of the missing Spitfires waited at the edge of the airstrip, eyes fixed on the direction they hoped the planes would return.

Nationalities never came into question; on adjacent wings within the 2nd TAF there were Polish, Dutch, Norwegian, Belgian, Canadian, New Zealand, Australian, and many other pilots including British whose planes were all being serviced and maintained by ground crews from various countries, who spoke many different languages. Within our own Free French squadron, the pilots, mostly French, came from as far afield as the Argentine to serve their country. I was responsible for the armament of a Spitfire called 'O for Olive'. For a short while, the pilot was a Luxemberger named Pierre. I felt a great personal loss when he failed to return on the last sortie of the day; one cannot really explain the bond that existed between the pilot and his ground crew.

As on previous moves we split into two groups, this time Tony Mattick was with me as the advanced echelon moved out from Vendeville. Dawn broke early that morning, very bright in the beginning but soon the sky became overcast with light rain. The long convoy of trucks first, followed by the heavy equipment with tractors, and Jeeps followed at the rear and the ever-present dispatch riders flashing backwards and forwards keeping contact with the moving crocodile of vehicles.

Our destination on this occasion was an airstrip just over the French border situated some four kilometres from the town of Menin in Belgium. The airstrip at Wevelgem had been used during the First World War for the fighter planes of that period.

On reaching the French-Belgian border the convoy travelled on into the town of Menin, where the welcome from the townsfolk was tremendous. As if from nowhere flowers appeared in the hands of small children.

When we reached the centre of Menin, I saw local people laying flowers on the town's memorial to the fallen from the First World War and as the column of vehicles turned right the road was crowded with people waving and cheering all the way until we entered Wevelgem and passed through the main entrance to the airstrip. Some few hours before, this airstrip had been occupied by the Luftwaffe and evidence of their hasty departure was everywhere. Our wing with the French squadrons, was to spend some ten weeks at Wevelgem and the many experiences that occurred there will always hold a very special place in the memories of the many ground crew who served on this airstrip during this period.

With the knowledge that our planes would soon be arriving from Vendeville, no time was lost in assembling all the equipment required to service them; flight mechanics, riggers, armourers, etc., suddenly came to life. Tents were soon erected and supplies of ammunition and bombs were stacked in dumps, near to where the aircraft would be dispersed when they landed.

Fortunately, as the aircraft began to arrive over the airstrip it began to rain again, and all operational sorties were cancelled. This at least gave the ground crews the opportunity to try and get organised.

About 20.00 hours that same evening, Tony Mattick and I decided to investigate the town of Menin. We both decided against leaving the airstrip by the main entrance and walking along the wall which was at the rear of our tents, we discovered a small subsidence which had obviously been made by the previous occupants of the airstrip. This was a hole sufficiently large enough for a person to squeeze themselves under the wall and out into the road outside. This particular exit was used extensively by many of the crews when leaving and returning to the airstrip during our stay at Wevelgem.

Once outside, we found ourselves very close to the tram terminal, where the trams ran to and from Wevelgem into Menin. These trams were the single deck variety with a large open platform at the rear of the tram, which contained any overspill of passengers from the interior.

Joining the tram, Tony and I soon arrived at Menin and were surprised to see all the lights on in the shops and cafés. On entering the first café we came to, it was soon very obvious that more than half the squadrons' ground crews all had the same idea, following various forms of exit from the airstrip and transportation into Menin.

After visiting several cafés, we found one which was larger than the rest, having a dance hall to the rear. Ordering two beers I found that as in the previous cafés the beer was fairly weak in fact the only way to give it body was to lace it with cognac. The fact that this café was packed did not seem to deter anyone from attempting to enter this establishment as there were a large number of local girls in attendance.

During the time I was at the bar, Tony had taken a fancy to a girl called Josephine who was seated at a nearby table. Her friend, who spoke English perfectly, introduced herself to me and said her name was Martha. Whilst Josephine was taller than Tony, she was also very volatile and spoke very little English. Martha was the complete opposite being quite small, dark and quietly spoken which suited me admirably as I could not stand noisy women.

In the weeks that followed Martha and I became very close friends, meeting as often as I was able to be off duty and leave the airstrip. Many times, Tony and Josephine would join us but as time went on, Tony found that his involvement with Josephine cut down any free time he had to wander around the cafés in Menin, which was what he loved to do.

I discovered that Martha was from a small village just outside Menin and was very much aware of our Squadron number. So much for security. During our evenings together she described the awful conditions that the town's people experienced living with the German Army in their town.

Menin – Wevelgem

As the opportunities arose Tony and me would leave the airstrip to travel into Menin for the evening and on one such occasion, to our dismay, we found that the trams had stopped running for the night. As there appeared to be no available transport, we decided to walk but had only gone a short distance from Wevelgem when a small civilian truck stopped and offered us a lift into Menin. The driver was a Belgian man and on our journey several times the truck came to a halt, the driver dismounted and proceeded to stoke up a small fire which was located just above the bonnet of the vehicle, this procedure was repeated until we arrived at Menin. Thanking the Belgian for the ride, both of us vanished into the nearest café to obtain a drink after this hilarious ride. It was only then did we discover that our faces were covered in coal dust that had surrounded our every stop on the journey into Menin.

It was on our many visits to the cafés in the town that Tony would, after a few drinks, get a glazed look into his eyes. I would then deliver him to where he had arranged to meet Josephine, sometimes later than the pre-arranged time. I would then meet Martha. At the end of the evening when it was time to return to the airstrip, my most difficult task was to find Tony. Menin, although a small town, contained many cafés and I often had to visit several cafés before I could locate him, then we would attempt to walk the four kilometres or so back to the airstrip – a task that sometimes took us both until the break of dawn.

During this period our Spitfires took on the role of fighter-bombers as against their normal role of giving air cover to the ground forces. This meant a 500lb bomb being suspended under the belly of the plane with 250lb bombs under each wing, a total of 1,000lb of high explosives in all.

On our squadron, as indeed the rest of the wing, the means of attaching the bombs to each plane was attained by sheer brute force as there was never any mechanical help available. Among the armourers on No. 341 Squadron were men who had been with the Free French squadrons since their formation at Turnhouse near Edinburgh. Their names easily came to mind, Jimmy (The Duke) Reed, Ken Griffiths, Bill (Tomo) Thompson, Walter (Timber) Wood, Jimmy Manaton, Tony (Mad) Mattick and many others. The fact that some eight sorties a day were being flown by the pilots also meant very long hours for the ground crews, irrespective of trade.

For the armourers, the only way to man-handle the bombs onto a Spitfire was for one armourer to kneel on all fours under the belly of the plane and two other armourers to lift the 500lb bomb onto the centre of the kneeling armourer's back and steady the bomb at the front and rear, while the armourer holding the bomb on his back attempted to lift the bomb upwards onto the retaining catch of a bomb carrier held underneath the aircraft. If luck was on your side, you managed to secure the bomb at the first attempt, although on many occasions it took several attempts to locate the retaining catch and secure the bomb.

After a day's flying combined with the normal servicing of both 20mm cannon and Browning ·5 machine guns, the opportunity to let off the tension of the day by a night out in Menin was often for many of us within the ground crews a chance to escape from the ever-present feeling of death and destruction.

As the weather kept fine, early morning sorties, often beginning at 04.30 hours, became standard procedure and the flight mechanics, riggers, armourers, instrument bashers and photographers would begin servicing the wing Spitfires at around 02.30 hours in preparation for the first take off.

The duration of each sortie, depending on the target, would vary between forty-five minutes and an hour. This increase in the number of sorties flown each day also increased the number of losses amongst the aircraft and pilots. On many occasions the aircraft did not make it back to the airstrip, but for those planes which did return the ground crews would wait and watch as several crash-landed with badly damaged aircraft and seriously wounded pilots.

It was not unusual for a Spitfire, badly shot up, trying to land at Wevelgem and in doing so crossing in front of other Spitfires circling the airstrip waiting in line to land. I can recall one such occasion when a Spitfire came in very quickly and tried to land in front of the other planes. I saw massive holes in the plane's fuselage and smoke coming from the engine; the pilot put the plane down without the undercarriage being lowered, resulting in the plane doing what we called a belly landing. As it came to a halt, smoke and flames engulfed the plane. Ground crews from all directions converged on the crashed plane but as the firefighters fought to get the blaze under control, others attempted to rescue the pilot from his blazing cockpit, although successful the pilot died of his wounds sometime later.

Many crashes that occurred during this very hectic period were quite horrific; another Spitfire returning to the airstrip, damaged and trying to land, crashed onto a photographic truck and was suspended on top of the truck. A ruptured petrol tank combined with the highly inflammable photographic material both the plane and the truck became a mass of flames. The pilot, injured and still strapped in his cockpit, was burnt to death, rescuers fought to reach him with ladders but were driven back by the heat and the flames.

On another occasion a Spitfire crash landed, slithered along the ground and came to rest with its cannons bent back like the trunk of an elephant, fortunately on this occasion the pilot walked safely away. I lost three pilots and Spitfires each being a replacement for O for Olive in one week. In two of the replacements I hardly got to know the new pilots before they were killed.

For all the ground crews of the squadrons it was a very difficult period, many of the flight mechanics and riggers would work for many hours in extremely arduous conditions trying to repair a badly damaged plane. It was therefore not unusual that when the opportunity arose to have few hours respite in Menin that the crews tried to put the tragic events of the days flying out of their minds. Although the beer was weak, laced with Cognac and the company of the local girls, one hoped to escape from this daily nightmare of contact with death.

Each day seemed to be worse than the previous day as the intensity of the sorties increased and the planes flew deeper into enemy airspace. The use of jettison petrol tanks became the order of the day. This meant that the longer the planes were flying the greater the chance of being hit by German anti-aircraft guns.

During the middle of September 1944, we saw a great armada of planes and gliders early one Sunday morning and at the time we wondered where the planes were heading. Little did we realise then that it was the prelude to the airborne drop over Arnhem. Later that day it began to rain quite heavily and continued to rain for over a week, and within hours the runways were like quagmires. Although we knew that aircover was needed in Arnhem our French wing and many of the other wings were grounded because of the inability to get the planes off the ground.

No flying of any consequence took place during that very tragic period. I can recall that with Ken Griffiths and Tony Mattick, we dug deep trenches around the outside of our tent in an effort to help to drain away the water that surrounded the tents. Everything that one seemed to possess was soaked with water.

It was so damp in the tents that ground crews attempted various forms of trying to dry out clothes and blankets. One group of flight mechanics in an adjacent tent took to heating up some loose bricks they had found with the aid of a blow lamp.

I think the worse part of this period was trying to eat our rations, as the field kitchens were a disaster, although in fairness the cooks working conditions were very difficult. After being on duty all through one night filling the petrol tanks of our entire squadron, plus loading the planes with bombs for a supposed early morning take off, the weather became worse again and we had the task of de-bombing the entire squadron.

It must have been around 05.00 hours when groups of various trades made their way towards the field kitchen and as it was still pouring with rain, we were all completely soaked to the skin. Our first sight of breakfast was to see food being cooked out in the open with the rain falling into the cooking pans, everything in our mess tin was afloat with water.

No one – unless they had served with an operational squadron in 2nd TAF – can comprehend the conditions that the ground crews had to live under whilst maintaining the planes in a first-class readiness state. Washing facilities for our mess tins were almost non-existent, just tubs of lukewarm water with lumps of fat floating on top. Most men preferred to clean their own mess tins with handfuls of grass, of which there was no shortage.

When it came to washing clothes, etc., one waited for a dry day, and removed all underclothes which were then dumped into a 14lb empty biscuit tin, two thirds full of water. Slices of soap were then thrown in and the tin was placed over a 'desert' fire. This comprised digging a large hole in the ground, with engine oil and petrol being poured into the hole and mixed with the loose earth. When this was sufficiently stirred to a muddy mess, one stood well back and set light to the contents. This method was guaranteed to burn for hours.

If you were fortunate, after hanging the contents of your laundry over the rigging lines of the tent, the articles of clothing would dry well enough for them to be worn again immediately. This process would be used over and over again and if you were last on the list, your underclothes came out a sight blacker than they went in.

Toilet arrangements were hilarious. Usually at some reasonable distance from the tents, three or four buckets were set in the ground and a small amount of hessian sack cloth would be supported by wooden poles as an aid to some privacy, however, not being very deep the heads and lower parts of the body could still be seen above and below the hessian screen. When the weather was bad and a force nine gale was blowing across the airstrip, anyone requiring use of the toilet facilities needed some form of anchor to maintain a level of balance. It was a natural outcome with the wing being stationed at Wevelgem for so many weeks that relationships began between members of the ground crew and the local girls from Menin, Wevelgem and Courtrai, including the many villages around the airstrip. Some of these relationships developed to such an extent that after the war ended, many of our ground crews returned to Belgium and married these local girls.

There were also one or two unpleasant aspects to some of these associations, in particular when a member of the ground crew was already married to a British girl back in England. Strange as it may seem, these men were often sent to Coventry, so to speak, by the rest of the ground crews.

One of the best remembered cafés in Menin, where many of these romances began was a large dance hall which was called the Felicepaleis, I remember meeting Martin there one evening. As usual it was packed with members of our squadrons, Jimmy Reed, The Duke was in his usual position at the end of the bar, his pipe glowing as red as ever, ably supported by Ken Griffiths, Bill Thompson (Tomo), Bob Pearson and several other armourers from 329, 340 and 341 squadrons.

One of our lads was celebrating his engagement to a local girl and the party went on until the very early hours. Finding myself pushed up against the bar, I began talking to a Belgian lad about my own age. He told me that his name was André Debael that he lived in Menin and was a (*Kleemaker*) (tailor) by trade. The fact that he spoke English very well enabled me to converse quite freely with him and from this meeting our friendship developed from then on. Later on, André invited me to his home in Menin where I met his parents and for the rest of my time at Wevelgem, André and I became close friends. On occasions when André and I met he would bring along a girlfriend and I would be accompanied by Martha, occasionally Tony Mattick and Josephine would join us but would move on when it appeared that Tony was getting that glazed look in his eyes.

Looking back, it all seems a very long time ago but my friendship with André Debael has stood the test of time, in so much that since the war I have returned to Belgium many times and have always visited André on each occasion. I know that I am not alone in my warm feelings for Wevelgem and Menin, in spite of the many terrible and horrendous things I was forced to witness on this airstrip as a young man. In the course of research, I have spoken to many former members of the ground crews of the French squadrons and found their feelings were similar to my own.

With regard to the lads who married local girls it must be said that they are indeed very forthright in their feelings, particularly as from those unions they have now grown-up sons and daughters.

Shortly before the end of October 1944, replacements for the Canadian division to whom we were giving continual air support began to move up towards the front line and one could hear the mixture of dialects, many of the young Canadians were of French extraction, and when they met our French pilots the meeting was a very warm and friendly occasion for all concerned. Unfortunately, the Canadians were to lose many of their number as they moved up towards Antwerp and the SS panzer divisions. We had attached to our squadron a Canadian liaison officer and for several days he was in constant contact with the ground forces and directed our Spitfires to where they could do the most damage to the German panzers. Our squadron flew sortie after sortie in low-level attacks with bombs fused with an instant 0·25 detonator in each bomb, sometimes the pilots went in at less than a height of 200 feet.

When the Canadians were eventually relieved, they told us that our pilots had dropped their bombs literally yards from the Canadian's dug outs in accurately bombing the German panzers.

One evening when most of the ground crews were in Menin, some of these Canadians sought out our squadron to thank us for the help we had given to them, apparently our pilots had taken their Spitfires in so low that the Canadians were easily able to see our squadron identification letters. Sadly, through this very hectic period we again suffered losses of both pilots and planes.

At the beginning of November, No. 340 Squadron returned to England and was replaced by No. 345 Free French squadron. We therefore had a few new faces amongst the French pilots. It was about this time, I noticed as dawn broke one morning a number of vapour trails high in the sky. I discovered later that they were V-2s on their way to London. At the time rumours of our impending move to Antwerp were abundant and as we were all aware of the V-2 attacks on the city, one could sense the general apprehension amongst the crews of the squadrons. Life continued to be extremely hectic with many sorties being flown, and the losses in planes were high with pilots killed and wounded. The ground crews worked in difficult conditions striving to keep their squadron Spitfires airborne and escaping at night to the cafés of Menin and Courtrai to find some solace in their brightly lit bars.

I found myself being an observer in seeing local Belgian men and women of all ages fighting to collect the contents of our mess tins which were emptied into refuse bins. To see this scene daily sickened me and many others, and to this day I have never forgotten the sight of those people fighting over scraps of food. We were not allowed to give food to the local people.

As had been rumoured for days, orders were received for the wing to move up to Duerne airstrip, near Antwerp, 25 November being the fateful day. Naturally the night of the 24th was spent by as many ground crews as duty would allow in Menin. For some of the lads with strong attachments, engaged, etc., to local girls it was surely an emotional time for them.

Entering the Felicepaleis in Menin on the last night, I found several of the armourers from the other squadrons, No. 329 and No. 345, and before long this café was so full that I decided to walk into the town. On my way out I passed Tony Mattick complete with Josephine, looking extremely the worst for the time of night. He was sitting at a table surrounded by armourers, Jimmy Reed (The Duke) as ever pipe glowing red was sat in one corner, whilst Ken Griffiths was in a heated conversation with Bill Thompson (Tomo) and Bob Pearson.

I think it was fair to say that the majority of the people in and around the town of Menin were much aware of our impending departure and also that the ground crews were very apprehensive of what was in store when the squadrons reached Antwerp. Bad news travels fast and we had already heard about the number of V-1s and V-2s which were dropping on this city and also the casualties amongst ground crews from other squadrons already operating from the Duerne airstrip.

As I wandered out into the main street of Menin I passed several cafés, each one seemed to have a full complement of crews from the squadrons. Walking further along the road, I stopped to look in the window of a local photographer named Wallecan. This man, over a period of some weeks, had taken many portrait photographs of different individual members of our ground crews, including me. Looking at the framed photographs I easily recognised many of the faces. I recall thinking how young we all seemed to appear, little did I realise at the time that some of the faces pictured in Wallecan's window would be dead within the month of their leaving Menin.

I had arranged to meet both André and Martha at the Felicepaleis, so I returned to the café and after a short time I was able to find André in the large crowd that had now filled the café. There was little we could say to one another, we were roughly the same age and had become close friends during my time in Wevelgem. I gave him some cigarettes and odd souvenirs, and said I would return once the war was over. I never appreciated then that our friendship would become so strong and continue for such a long time. Martha, hearing that I had returned to the café, soon joined me and eventually finding a seat I found that Tony was as usual well inebriated.

Some of the lads were beginning to make their way back to Wevelgem, knowing full well that they would have to walk the whole distance as the trams had long since ceased to operate. When it came to say goodbye to Martha, I found it difficult to say a great deal except that I would write to her when I reached Antwerp. She asked me whether I was afraid, I replied that like the rest of the lads, I was scared and yet had to go irrespective of what fate had in store for me. With hindsight some thirty-five years on, I have come to the same conclusion as many ex-ground crews did, that it seems a hell of a waste of young human life.

As it was now getting quite late, I said my last farewells to André and Martha and with Tony now ably supported by Josephine, we made our way towards the main road back to camp. It was rather an emotional parting for Tony and Josephine but nevertheless for Tony, I believe, it was a welcome relief. After a very long and difficult walk along the cobbled road we at last staggered into our tent on reaching camp. My own feelings at the time were once we had left Wevelgem, none of our lives would ever really be the same.

For me this was completely true.

During my time at Wevelgem, I like, many of my friends, spent the evenings when duty allowed in and around the cafés in Menin and I have some pleasant memories of evenings spent in this town. The two most popular songs of the day were firstly one called *Fascination* and secondly *Opus One*; they were beamed to the Allied troops in Europe by the American Forces Network.

It goes without saying that over the years following the end of the war that whenever I hear either of these tunes, my thoughts turn to the café called Felicepaleis in Menin and the airstrip at Wevelgem. The song called *Fascination* was to be very important to me towards the end of 1945 and even now thirty-five years on.

Chapter 8

Duerne near Antwerp (The Hell Hole)

The long convoy of vehicles moved slowly out from the airstrip at Wevelgem onto the hard cobbled road leading towards Sourtrsi. As previous it was a leap-frogging operation with skeleton ground crew left behind until the main force reached Duerne near Antwerp.

Once all the aircraft had taken off for the last time at Wevelgem, the token crews would pack up everything and then re-join the squadrons at Duerne. I can say with certainty that many of the crews had very little if any sleep, mainly because of the early hour we left the airstrip. Some of the lads were fortunate not to be left behind as they arrived very late back from Menin, looking very much the worse for their night's endeavours.

Again, Tony and I were in the first section with several other armourers. The Duke, Ken Griffiths, Tomo, Timber Wood, Jimmy Manaton, Sid Shupick and a few others were in the group that remained.

Passing through several small Belgian villages we continued on towards Antwerp. After leaving Ghent I pointed out to the rest of the occupants of the truck the ominous vapour trails of the V-2 rockets. At that time, it did not seem to matter a great deal but within a short distance we did not have to wait very long before Hitler's promise to wipe Antwerp off the map was a real threat indeed. Several times the convoy was forced to stop with the crews diving out of the trucks and finding whatever cover they could as V-1 rockets droned overhead. When the rocket engines cut out, it was only a matter of a few seconds before the rocket went into a low dive followed by a terrific explosion.

On one such occasion, I watched a V-1 droning overhead with the flames from the rocket engine lighting up the sky. This time it was right above our truck and I watched, almost transfixed, hoping, willing this terrible weapon to keep going and not cut out above me. Fortunately, it came down a few seconds later but still close enough to shake my teeth and set my ears ringing with the force of the explosion. At that precise moment I did not think that there were any non-believers amongst any of us sheltering on the ground.

The bombardment became more intense as we entered the confines of Antwerp and the evidence of the damage by the German V-1s and V-2s was very plain to see, Tony Mattick remarked at the time, 'This is where we really get hit' and no one in our truck was prepared to argue the point.

Having arrived at the Duerne airstrip, I discovered that it had concrete runways. These were certainly a change from the grass runways that the squadron had previously operated from. However, the place was a hive of activity as several other squadrons were also operating from this airstrip. Thundering Tiffys (Typhoons) were roaring along the runway heading towards the front line a few miles away.

Meanwhile every few minutes the sirens would start wailing indicating that more V-1s were overhead and to seek cover. The first dash to cover I made with Tony was behind a huge mound, it was only when the 'all clear' sounded that I discovered we had been seeking cover behind a large number of 500lb bombs being made ready for use that day.

Shortly after establishing where our wing had been allocated space on the airstrip, we saw our Spitfires circling overhead and soon they proceeded to land. They were quickly re-fuelled and re-armed, and were soon airborne again heading in the same direction as the Typhoon squadrons.

The V-1s continued to appear above us all day, some falling on the airstrip where they invariably caused casualties amongst ground crews sited around the perimeter of the airstrip. The rapidity of their arrival seemed to me like a bus terminal, endless.

With daylight failing, our Spitfires began to circle the airstrip landing one by one, on this last sortie of the day two planes were missing, an omen of worst to come. Tony and I, along with several of our crews began to make our way towards a small block of flats in the near vicinity of the airfield. Carrying what kit we could manage, we arrived at these unoccupied civilian flats. 'Good Lord', said Tony upon entering the hallway, 'Someone's gone off his rocker to give us billets like these'.

As the rest of the crews followed into this three-storey block of flats there was a mad rush to investigate the rest of the accommodation. I discovered there were several toilets which actually flushed and a bathroom. The only disadvantage was that the Germans who had been the previous tenants had in their withdrawal from Duerne removed all the taps, toilet seats and chains, why they should need such articles was a complete mystery.

Duerne near Antwerp (The Hell Hole)   159

However, the noise coming from the rooms above was appalling as it appeared that everyone was trying out the toilets at the same time. Privacy did not exist when everybody was accustomed to sleeping and resolving their toilet and washing facilities out in the open countryside. The added bonus of having electricity throughout the building combined with the ingenuity of the electricians among the crews, soon made life somewhat bearable.

Having established a place in one of the rooms to make up a bed, Tony and I made our way back towards the airfield in search of something to eat. On entering the mess, I was amazed by the large murals to be seen everywhere on the mess walls and ceilings. All the murals appeared to be depicting the German slogan of 'Strength Through Sex', voluptuous blonde figures completely nude in various poses with tall blonde male figures, exhibiting their genital organs for all to see. At the time I thought what an aperitif to our first meal since leaving Wevelgem.

Returning to our civilian billets someone had managed to heat sufficient water for a bath, however, as there had been several bathers before me the colour of the water was a little cloudy to say the least. Nevertheless the opportunity to have a bath was too good to miss, although one of our previous occupants had penned a notice to the bathroom wall suggesting that 'Bathers should not stir the mud in the bottom of the bath'.

Tony followed my lead and entered the bath as I came out. During this time the bombardment of V-1s and V-2s continued and it was with somewhat of a shock that I heard the crashing of glass coming from the bathroom. Hearing the cursing coming from Tony, I ran up to the bathroom to be greeted with the sight of Tony sitting in the bath but completely covered in plaster and rubbish which had come down on top of him as he attempted to carry out his ablutions.

It appeared that one of the many explosions had brought down a glass skylight narrowly missing Tony, but the rest of the plaster roof had collapsed onto him. Once over the shock of seeing him still alive. I was convulsed with laughter at the sight he presented to me and the other so-called rescuers.

Later in the evening as things had quietened down, I suggested that we should find a café. Feeling quite refreshed Tony and I had only walked a few doors away from the billet when we came upon a café aptly named 'The Welcome'. On entering I soon found that the ground crew from our billet were already well established at the bar and as in most cafés there was the usual number of Belgian girls in the Welcome café. We had hardly ordered a beer, when there was a violet explosion quite close, resulting in the front door and windows of the café being blown innermost. For a while some confusion reigned and everyone seemed covered in dust and debris but eventually people picked themselves off the floor, the door was placed back on its hinges and things got back to normal.

The continual noise of explosions carried on but perhaps because of the effect of the alcohol, the fear I had first experienced slowly receded. Tony, never slow to make friends with girls, soon found himself a suitable companion and after a short period, I realised that Josephine back in Wevelgem had long since been forgotten. I cannot recall the time we eventually got to bed but it seemed an awful long day since leaving Wevelgem.

Before dropping off, I promised myself that I would write to Martha the next day.

Our second day at Duerne began with a glorious bright sunny day and very soon all three French squadrons were airborne, a prelude to a very busy day. We did not have long to wait before the Spitfires returned, some with flak holes and looking like giant pepper pots, where the flack had been heavy. No losses this time, thank goodness, a quick check for damage, re-fuel, re-arm and away the fighters went again. Soon the V-1s and V-2s appeared once again. Nobody seemed to bother about this at first until the huge black palls of smoke, followed by massive explosions as the rockets started to drop onto the airstrip, it wasn't the time to hang about admiring the scenery. Just after lunchtime the rest of the crews arrived from Wevelgem, I remember Ken Griffiths asking me, how bad were things at Duerne, 'bloody awful', I replied.

After a few days it was decided to give a few ground crews time off to go to Antwerp. One such group of armourers visiting a cinema in the town were very lucky to escape with their lives. Shortly after entering the cinema a V-1 crashed on the opposite side of the road. Such was the devastation that no one knew where to look for the crew.

However, although badly bruised and shaken up, they survived. I remember one of the armourers nicknamed 'Edna' Coleman walking towards me, with blood running down under his chin. On closer inspection I saw that he had a series fine pin holes under his chin which gave the impression that his throat had been cut. Fortunately, it wasn't that serious but nevertheless this episode quietened everybody down for the rest of the day.

During my time in France and Belgium, I had on many occasions wondered how the various trades which made up ground crews managed to maintain such a high standard of serviceability in keeping the aircraft continually flying. The conditions under which the flight mechanics made not only minor but major overhauls to the engines of the planes, working mostly out in the open and subject to the extremes of the weather was indeed quite remarkable. This also applied to the riggers, armourers, electricians and all the many other tradesmen. Although very strong rivalry existed between the different trades there also existed a very deep bond within any squadron ground crew.

Over the years, I have not seen a great deal written which emphasized the tremendous effort which the vast number of ground crews throughout the RAF and the 2nd TAF gave in supporting the air crews of the various Bomber, Fighter and Coastal Command squadrons.

As the bombardment of Antwerp and our airstrip at Duerne continued, the daily sorties of the fighters appeared to increase in number. On one of the early morning sorties, our squadron was taking off when the Spitfire 'O' for Olive which I was responsible for had just lifted from the runway when the 500lb bomb carried under the belly of the plane dropped from the plane and came to rest on the concrete runway. Within seconds the siren began to wail and red Very lights were fired into the air, at the same time the ground crew took cover.

Amongst our group of armourers, we had one called Bob Mackenzie ('Mac') a Scot and well-liked by everyone. I remember he jumped into a Bedford truck and called to me to join him. As we headed onto the runway, I felt a terrible fear that the bomb would explode at any time as we approached it. We both alighted from the truck and walked towards the bomb and on examination I noticed that although the tail fin was badly damaged the arming pistols in the front and rear of the bomb were still intact and that their securing pins were still in place not, as I had imagined, been left attached to the plane.

Whilst Mac reversed the truck along the runway, I waited with the bomb and with a great deal of effort we managed to manhandle the bomb onto the back of the vehicle, Mac drove very carefully back towards our bomb dump, whilst I held the bomb secure in the back of the vehicle. Once arrived the bomb was unloaded and quickly defused.

Whether it was the effort or the fear but for the rest of the day I was in a complete daze, Tony Mattick commented on seeing me, that I looked like a ghost. There was a small enquiry which proved nothing and the whole matter was passed over, although for Bob Mackenzie and me it was quite some time before we could put the incident out of our minds.

Later that same night on entering the Welcome café I was the target for some well-meaning ribald comments from my fellow armourers. Tony trying to cheer me up bought me several cognacs and slowly as the alcohol took effect the fear and the coldness I was experiencing gradually subsided.

The café was unusually full this night and as previously Tony found some female companions, the two Belgian girls thinking I was ill asked what was wrong with me, Tony said quite seriously, 'He's just dropped a bomb'.

From what I recall of that evening it turned out to be one of the noisiest, as several V-1s landed in the very near vicinity of the café and the door kept being blown off its hinges.

It was the following morning that a V-1 crashed onto the runway; this time closer to our squadron than previous explosions. Fortunately, it came down when the majority of the ground crews were in the mess hall. However, the skeleton crew on duty were caught in the blast, several of them receiving shrapnel wounds although one corporal of an adjacent squadron was killed outright. From then on the bombardment of the airstrip seemed to increase daily, although one could see in the early morning light the endless rockets heading in the direction of London. The strain of operating on the airstrip with the V-1s and V-2s continually bombarding us was beginning to take its toll on the ground crews. At night it was impossible to sleep because of the endless explosions which occurred, therefore most nights the crews would seek some relief in the many cafés around the airstrip.

One evening I thought I would answer some letters, so I walked down to the perimeter of the airstrip and entered the hangar where our armourers' truck was parked inside. Climbing into the cab of the truck I began to write to my mother. Suddenly I sensed a coldness throughout my body which I could not account for, in fact the whole of the hangar seemed quite eerie. Leaving the truck, I walked outside onto the airstrip and the coldness disappeared, after some fifteen minutes I returned to the hangar and almost immediately I began to feel this odd and cold sensation. The whole episode was extremely frightening to me, and I felt quite disturbed by this experience and decided to return to the billet where I was able to finish writing my letters.

On leaving the billet I went along to the Welcome café and found as usual Tony enjoying the female company at his table, on seeing me, he laughingly remarked 'You look as if you've just seen a bloody ghost'. At the time Tony's comment did not really mean anything, though towards the end of December 1944, I was to remember that hangar at Duerne and the feeling of coldness, I felt on that particular evening.

As the ground crews began to enter the café it wasn't long before the armourers seem to congregate around several tables. Ken Griffiths accompanied by the faithful Jimmy (The Duke) Reed, Tomo Thompson, Bob Pearson, Sid Shupick, Timber Wood, Jimmy Manaton, Bob (Mac) Mackenzie, Pete Markham, Edna Coleman and many other armourers were all well away when I first joined them and I wasn't long before my experience at the hangar slowly faded from my mind.

The explosions from the V-1s and V-2s landing around Antwerp were still continuing and I had just commented that Duerne appeared quieter than normal when one of the loudest explosions occurred near the café. The result was chaos for some minutes as everyone was covered in dust and debris and most of the occupants of the café finished up on the floor. It took some time to sort things out and to put the place back in some kind of order but eventually as things got back to normal the laughter and ribald comments took over again and the evening continued.

However, shortly after midnight a call came for the ground crews to report to the dispersal points as a gale was forecast and the Spitfires were moving about the airstrip. As we left the café it began to snow, nothing is more soul destroying than to try and tighten rigging lines holding the Spitfires on the parked dispersal points particularly when the rigging is wet with snow. It took best part of the night to secure all the canvas covers and to batten down everything moveable. By this time, I was beginning to feel like an iceberg and Tony's nose was glowing a glorious red.

As the ground crews made their way towards the mess hall to get some hot tea which scalded the throat but helped to thaw out the frozen hands, gradually one began to feel the warmth returning to the body. Dawn was just breaking as we walked back towards the billet and Tony looking up at the sky, commented to me 'We have seemed to have seen an awful lot of dawns break'.

The crews had a brief respite and then back to the airstrip, as we arrived the overnight snow was being cleared away from the runways. I looked at Jimmy Reed with his pipe ever glowing, he managed a grin as I walked towards 'O' for Olive the Spitfire I was responsible for.

The telephone soon jingled in the flight tent and soon the pilots ran towards their respective planes, taking off in threes as they scrambled to gain height. I looked around at the rest of the armourers, all appeared strangely quiet, perhaps like me they were still feeling the effects of the previous night's efforts. It turned out to be a very busy day with several Spitfires and Typhoons crashing on returning to Duerne and we had some losses, replacements arriving within a matter of hours complete with pilots.

The light was beginning to fail as I joined Ken Griffiths and helped him re-service his aircraft and with the other armourers

Duerne near Antwerp (The Hell Hole) 167

began to return to the billet. Both Tony and I along with Bob Pearson and Mac were the on-duty crew for the night, so we had a quick meal in the mess hall and just sat around in the crew room on the airstrip watching the endless V-1s and V-2s some heading for Antwerp, others higher up, obviously heading towards London.

About 21.00 hours the same evening the telephone began to ring in the Duty Officers' building and then we had activity plus. A very early morning sortie for the three squadrons was ordered from Headquarters, to give air cover to the Canadian division advancing into Holland the following day. Out onto the dispersal ran the flight mechanics, riggers, armourers, etc., to service and to re-arm and bomb up some thirty-six Spitfires. Very soon the bomb trolleys arrived depositing a 500lb and 250lb bombs just in front of each aircraft.

To bomb up an aircraft in daylight can be very hazardous but at night a mistake can be fatal. We had just begun when again snow started to fall, lightly at first then a real blizzard took over. As we struggled, our task became extremely difficult mainly because of the dreadful weather combined with our heavy cumbersome outer clothing.

It proved to be a very long night and soon the darkness was lit as the flight mechanics revved up the engines of the Spitfires, which caused great flames to stretch out past the sides of the planes from the exhausts, lighting up the faces of all around. As the mechanics revved up the engines to 18lb boost, alternate ground crews would sit on the tail section holding onto each other as the engines roared and the planes vibrated. It was quite an experience, although the noise deafened you for some minutes afterwards. Eventually having completed the servicing of all the three squadrons the crews stood around in groups. By this time the snow had ceased to fall and people were clearing the snow from the concrete runways.

A vivid red sky broke the dawn and soon the pilots were arriving for their briefing. Apparently some SS panzers were giving the Canadian division a rough time in a heavily wooded area near the Dutch border this side of Eindhoven. Taking off immediately, the Spits circled the airstrip once before climbing towards the watery sun now showing itself.

Taking the opportunity, Tony and I decided to get some breakfast as the planes would soon be returning. The hot food helped and, as the crews began to relax, I sensed a feeling of confidence from the men around me concerning the previous night's efforts.

Looking around the mess hall I saw most of the duty crews from the various squadrons stationed at Duerne. They all looked very much the same, tired, dirty and with red noses, but laughter began to come at first in quiet guffaws, then great roars of laughter as the tales of the nights funny stories began to be told. I did not feel I was particularly patriotic but the knowledge that I was a member of these men who made up the ground crews, made me feel very proud indeed; this was the *esprit de corps* within the 2nd TAF.

Arriving back at dispersal we soon saw the first planes, just dots at first, then we could identify the different planes: B for Bertie, U for Uncle, F for Freddie and so on. A couple of Spits did a victory roll over the airstrip before coming into land. On this sortie all our planes were back safely. We quickly re-armed

Duerne near Antwerp (The Hell Hole)   169

and re-fuelled the planes as other crews checked the aircraft. I had a brief conversation with my pilot and a cigarette and then he was back into the cockpit, a quick thumbs up and a wave and away the planes went again. This continued for another six sorties and then our squadron was stood down for twenty-four hours. At the end of the day, we had lost four Spitfires from our squadron, one pilot was safe having managed to bale out and land in our lines, whilst the other three were seen to go down in flames over enemy territory. The pilot of my Spitfire, a young Frenchman not much older than me called Henri, was one of the three who failed to return from this sortie. Tony, Ken Griffiths, and Mac waited with me at the edge of the runway after the majority of the aircraft had landed. I listened for a sound of an engine hoping that my 'O' for Olive would suddenly appear in the darkening sky. After some thirty minutes our wing commander walked towards us and gave me the bad news.

That night everybody was a little quiet by normal standards, a reaction following the deaths of the three young pilots. All our ground crews seemed to take the loss very hard. I recall thinking 'here today gone tomorrow'. It was depressing to go into the mess hall as other squadrons from our 145 Wing had also suffered losses and the place reminded me of a wake. Walking back to the billet, I said to some of the lads, 'let's get the hell out of it and go into Antwerp for the night'. 'Great' said Tony.

Quickly changing into a clean uniform about twenty of us scrounged a lift into Antwerp and it did not take long to find a suitable bar to start a pub crawl. There was nothing different inside the café compared to any other café except that it had half doors which swung backwards and forwards as you passed through, just like the doors in the Westerns in American films. The reason for the unusual doors soon became obvious a little later on, when a disturbance began at the bar between some Army lads and some other servicemen. As the fighting began several large civilians appeared as from nowhere and waded into the melee. It was then I understood the reason for the half swing doors, as the originators of the argument were thrown ignominiously through the doors to land in a heap on the pavement outside the café. Just like John Wayne, I thought at the time.

Having witnessed the inglorious exit of the Army lads, Tony, me, and the others in our party decided it was time we left as quietly as possible. I don't think any of us relished the thought of flying like a sack of potatoes through the sturdy half doors.

Moving onto another café, I noticed that the lads in our party were starting to relax, and the depression seemed to be lifting from us as the alcohol took over. Tony was by this time eyeing up the attractive girls, and I found that the lads were splitting up into small groups, before long we appeared to have taken over most of the café.

I found myself separated from Tony and began talking to a Belgian girl, whilst Jimmy Reed, Ken and Tomo were with another group of girls at the other end of the bar. The rest of our lads were dotted about the place at various tables all with female company. As time passed the place became noisier and as more of our ground crews entered the café it became packed to capacity.

Just after midnight I was beginning to feel the effects of the past days efforts and combined with the beer I had consumed,

I knew that I would soon fall asleep if I stayed at the café and it was obvious that several lads felt the same way. Tony was very unsteady on his feet and as we pulled Jimmy Reed to his feet, he appeared to be worse than any of us, his nose was bright red and with his pipe firmly fixed between his teeth, he looked a sorry sight.

With Bob Mackenzie one side of him and Ken Griffiths on the other side we left the café. Although somewhat depleted from our original number, our intention was to walk back to the airstrip at Duerne. Fortunately, we were able to secure a lift in one of our squadron trucks en route back to Duerne. None of us being very sober, the journey became quite hilarious but arriving eventually at our billets Jimmy Reed was carried in and put to bed and one of my fondest memories of The Duke was the sight of him in bed complete with his pipe still in his mouth. I recall at the time that his bosom friend Ken Griffiths, who was easily stirred into wild hysterics at any time, being almost paralytic with laughter at the normally solemn Duke quoting lines from William Shakespeare.

On reflection, the time our squadrons spent operating from the Duerne airstrip near Antwerp was perhaps the most dangerous and devastating from the ground crews' point of view. As I have already mentioned the crews were made up of many various trades and in 341 Squadron the majority of individual men's surnames were never used. We had an armourer, Flight Sergeant Feeney known as 'Chiefy', and a Sergeant Knott known affectionately as 'Lofty' Knott; many armourers had a nickname. We had 'Chalky' White and 'Timber' Wood. Another lad, whose surname I can never remember, was known simply as 'Snozzle'; his success at finding a girl anywhere we travelled was his greatest asset. Bob Mackenzie was known as 'Mac', Bill Thompson was 'Tomo' and Jimmy Reed was called 'The Duke'. Amongst the corporals we had Tony Mattick known as 'Mad Mattick', Pollard was called 'Polly' and Neish was 'Neishy'.

This use of nicknames also applied to the flight mechanics, riggers, etc. Our photographer was known as 'Wee Jock Crawford', although many names have with the passing of time escaped my memory. One mechanic whose name is well known and remembered by many of the ground crews was Corporal George Blaikie, he had served with the Free French squadrons since their original formation and had quite recently been recognised by the French Government for his service to the Free French Air Force during 1940-1945 and received an appropriate award.

I remember the ground crews I was involved with as a wonderful group of men, unorthodox in their dress but fiercely protective within their own group or trade. They were extremely loyal and proud of the French squadrons, the French pilots, and the Spitfires that they maintained. A motley crowd, perhaps, from varying civilian backgrounds but thrown together by the circumstances of war.

During the period the ground crews were at Duerne, everyone endeavoured to stay alive but with the continual bombardment of V-1s and V-2s which had increased since the French squadrons arrived taking its daily toll of death or injury among the ground crews. One could see the effect this was having on the men's attitudes and the chance to escape at night to the cafés and bars around the airstrip gave some relief, plus the fact that there were always unlimited numbers of Belgian girls quite willing to listen to the men's problems and fears. Bravado often became the order of the night as men told each other that they were not scared.

As the daily sorties went on, orders were received for some of the ground crews to travel in trucks into Holland in an attempt to retrieve the ammunition and petrol which was stored on some advanced airstrips. Reports of German troops making a counterattack to capture these stores were quickly passed by word of mouth and those crews who were sent into Holland returned with stories of the devastation they had seen.

It was the following day, 8 December 1944, that Bob Mackenzie and I were ordered to report to the Squadron Headquarters. Leaving the dispersal point we made our way to headquarters, I felt very apprehensive but not prepared for the news that Mac and I had been posted back to England. We were ordered to leave Antwerp the next morning. Apparently we had both been seconded to a composite squadron which was being relieved and returning for a rest to England. Both Mac and I were so surprised by this news that it took a little time for us to realise that the war in Europe could be over for us.

Returning to the squadron our news swiftly went around the crews and when the last sortie of the day had been flown, I returned to the billet to begin to pack my kit.

Mad Mattick, Ken Griffiths and The Duke had been in Antwerp most of the day therefore the news of Mac and I returning to England came as quite a shock to them when they entered the billet. All four of us had been through quite a lot together and in particular Tony and I had been together since I first joined 341 FF Squadron and the thought of my returning to England without him wasn't a happy prospect, however I promised Tony that if I got leave, I would visit his family at Tilehurst near Reading.

That evening turned out to be quite a memorable occasion as half the squadron ground crews joined Mac and me in the Welcome Café to celebrate our departure for England the following day. Tony got quite drunk and Jimmy Reed, whose record was some 16 pints, appeared to be in a world of his own with a glorious red nose and the pipe firmly in place.

The café did some brisk business on the night particularly as more of the off-duty crews joined in the celebrations. During the latter part of the evening Mac was doing some form of highland jig surrounded by fellow Scots completely oblivious to the continual explosions that carried on throughout the night.

Just after midnight Mac and I decided to get our heads down as we had to leave very early in the morning. As we both left the café with all the good wishes of the crews, I must admit I felt somewhat sad to have to leave without Tony who was sitting with a Belgian girl at a table near the door of the café looking completely shattered. As I passed, he said to me, 'Good Luck Ron, tell my folks I am okay'. Sadly, it was the last time I ever saw Tony Mattick.

When at last I got to bed I felt a relief at the thought of returning to England away from so much death and destruction, never knowing whether the next V-1 or V-2 had my number on it and I would not be honest if I did not admit to being scared every day I had been at the Duerne airstrip.

I know I wasn't alone with my fears, many times I had seen men with the grey pallor of plain fear when an explosion had been too close for comfort. The next morning, I went in search of Bob Mackenzie and when I found him, he looked very much the worst for wear. We made our way to headquarters where we joined a group of other ground crews from several different squadrons. In all we had approximately 175 ground crews, a couple of NCOs and a very young officer who had recently arrived from England.

After a short time, a line of trucks appeared and throwing my kit into the first one Mac and I climbed into the back of the truck and very soon the convoy moved out, leaving behind the skyline of Antwerp which slowly disappeared into the distance.

Later that day, the convoy arrived at an empty school house on the outskirts of Ostend, our departure point. We spent the night in the school sleeping on the stone floors. I still remember looking towards Antwerp that night and being able to see clearly the V-1s and the V-2s still exploding in and around the city. I thought to myself, 'Thank God, I am out of that hell hole.' Apart from the draughts I slept well, and Mac and I awoke to a brilliant sunny day, breakfast was hard rations and we re-joined the trucks which took us to Ostend harbour.

Although an LCT was taking on stores, nobody in the Navy seemed to know anything about us and we were forced to hang about for some time until the powers that be decided who we were, and the Navy agreed to transport us to England.

As Mac and I found ourselves a bunk each, I lay back and thought, marvellous, England ahead, thank God.

Personal account of V-2 Rocket Attack on 20 December 1944 at Duerne Airstrip near Antwerp which decimated No. 341 Free French Squadron, 145 Wing 2nd Tactical Air Force. Exactly as set down in a letter to the author by:
Ex Corporal George Blaikie. Fitter Airframes.
No. 341. Free French Squadron.
Awarded the *Médaille de l'Aéronautique* 1945.

I certainly remember each individual rocket (V-2s) which almost wiped out 341 FF Squadron. I was going back to the flights after tea when it happened. I was too near to hear any noise, it did something to my ears and I was thrown off the perimeter onto the grass verge between two Spits (the V-2 had landed on the aerodrome and dug in deep and blew high). I was staggering around and there was earth and stones dropping all around me; there was a mist and I couldn't see where I was. My cap was away, I had on a leather jerkin and I was trying to put one end over my head as I had suffered a bad head injury at Drem in 1943 and I was trying to save my head. However, the smoke and mist cleared up and I looked around, found that my left leg was in a hole in the ground and the water was running over the top of my gumboot, filling the inside of the boot.

I picked up my cap and my knees were knocking, I could also see that the majority of the aircraft had been badly damaged, some had their backs broken. The IFF had detonated with the blast, then I saw the guard parade – it was a right shambles. Then out of the blue up came a jeep and a Flight Lieutenant was driving. His forehead was bleeding. He asked me, 'What squadron Corporal?'

I said, 'What's left of this one'.

He said, 'What trade?'

I said 'Airframe'.

He replied, 'Fine I am the new DSO, check all aircraft and let me know how many will be serviceable. We will need twelve in the morning.'

I said, 'What about the lads lying injured over there?'

He said, 'There's plenty of bods can do that but none can do your job.' I was very pleased that I had something to do as my knees were still shaky.

We had only eight out of twenty-one aircraft serviceable; we worked all night and made another two serviceable, borrowed two Spitfires from another squadron and we had twelve at the ready in the morning.

I was in the canteen when the second V-2 landed at teatime. I had a mug of tea in my hand and was just sitting down when all the tables and chairs all flattened, and I was sitting on the floor. I thought that's us again, and when I went onto the flight there was just a big hole, everything else had just vanished.

Later that week a V-1 came over the drome the engine cut out, the nose dropped, it seemed to be coming for the squadron and none of us could move. Then the engine seemed to pick up again and veered away to the right onto the far end of the aerodrome exploding on an anti-aircraft gun site.

Letter from George Blaikie Esq.

I was informed whilst I was still in Germany in 1945 that the authorities had checked up and discovered that out of the whole of No. 145 Wing which contained over 1500 ground crews on maintenance and the flights, there were only three men who had been with the Free French from when No. 340. F. F. Squadron was formed in December 1941. Two were officers and I was the only N.C.O. We were awarded the 'Médaille de l'Aéronautique' [in] 1945. I received the award in 1949 and also a mention in 1946 for what had happened at Duerne, Antwerp, in the first of the V-2 incidents in December 1944.

Whilst I was with No. 340 F.F. Squadron at Hornchurch the whole squadron was awarded the 'Croix du Guerre' and it was pinned on the squadron flag, following the Dieppe landings of August 12th 1942.

In January 1945, No. 341 F.F. Squadron was awarded the 'Croix du Guerre' and it was pinned on No. 341's Squadron flag at Duerne, Antwerp, following the incidents on the 20th December 1944. The ceremony took place where the flight office had been and where the pilots, armourers, and many other trades from the ground crews were killed.

The French have awarded me the 'Fererragere Croix du Guerre 1939–1945'.

In July 1944, I saw Boudier going off on a sweep from Selsey and he was shot down. At the time our C.O. Capitaine Martell was very upset over the loss of Boudier.

However, at the end of March 1945 when the squadron was stationed at the Schinjdel airstrip in Holland, I was repairing a Spit, when I heard a voice say, 'Are you still with us Jock?' and it turned out to be Boudier. He had been in a P.O.W. camp and was released when the Russians advanced into that part of Germany and was on his way back to find his family in France.

George Blaikie,
Ex Corporal No. 341 Free French Squadron
No. 145 Wing, 2nd Tactical Air Force

Chapter 9

England Ahead (Fairwood Common)

As the LCT left the harbour at Ostend and headed out into the English Channel it tended to wallow and, because of the rolling motion, the majority of the men with this composite servicing echelon began to feel the effects of the rolling sensation caused by the turbulent state of the sea.

I myself felt that I was in a barrel and when lunch time came around only about a third of our complement bothered to leave their bunks and climb the metal stairs to the ship's galley above them. Those, including me, who queued up on deck to enter the galley were greeted with the terrible unappetizing smell of Irish stew being served from tins complete with hard biscuits, this being standard operational rations.

However, many lads just couldn't face it and the ever-present seagulls had a birthday as the dixies of stew were thrown overboard. The evening meal fared the same way, although I was more fortunate than most as I had a tin of corned beef in my kit and, with some bread I acquired from one of the cooks by means of barter, at least Mac and I had something solid to eat. By this time most people were feeling pretty awful, and many were seasick as the ship was being thrown about quite a bit. Around midnight a gale began to blow and, as the lads became ill, the rush to use the ship's toilets was continuous.

Unfortunately, these services were extremely limited which tended to aggravate the situation.

I slept fairly well in spite of the moans and groans and when the ship's loudspeakers boomed out, 'Troops to breakfast', Mac and I made our way once again up to the ship's galley, although Mac was looking very sickly. It was still blowing hard, and we were met with driving rain as we queued on deck, shuffling along until we gratefully entered the confines of the warm galley. Once inside the sight of tinned American fat bacon being emptied into giant frying pans was too much for Mac who took off in the direction of the nearest rail and spent some minutes prostrated over the side of the ship. As he returned, he saw that I had a mess tin containing what could only be described as snakes and ladders, Mac took one look and promptly returned to his stance at the ships rail. Eventually we both returned to our bunks, where Mac rolled onto the bed and suggested that he was dying.

Owing to the heavy seas and the fact that some mines had broken loose we were forced to spend another night in the English Channel. The next morning when all was clear we entered the harbour at Tilbury, and I was pleased to stand once more on terra firma.

As we disembarked, I must admit we looked more like a group of PoWs as very few of the men were dressed in RAF uniform. Apart from our young officer the majority were wearing a mixture of khaki uniform and civilian clothes. I was still wearing an army battledress with a series of bullet holes running at a forty-five-degree angle across the front of the blouse, which left no one in doubt as to the previous owner's war service. Hideous perhaps, but the army, having retrieved and laundered the uniforms, felt in their wisdom, 'waste not want not'.

We came as a great shock to the regimental sergeant major of the army at Tilbury when he mistook us for a bunch of 'Bloody Jerries' and cursed us accordingly. He was even more infuriated when it was pointed out to him by our young officer that we were not only British but Allies.

I felt that the regimental sergeant major must have blown a fuse when he saw this load of all nation ruffians, all having been operational and veterans of the war come trooping off the ship. Many of our group were of different nationalities, some were Polish, Belgian, French, Dutch, Norwegian and British. I thought at the time that we rather resembled 'Bassetts Allsorts' with a language problem.

As we were handed over to the army, no one seemed to know what to do with us, we received breakfast which we ate under some converted railway arches. When lunchtime arrived, we were given some cold rations but as the camp was being used for embarking soldiers for Europe, we found that the army officers kept on mistaking us for army because of our khaki battledress, and everything seemed to be chaotic.

The weather at the time was appalling it was raining continuously and we were allocated some Bell tents but no blankets, just a few duck boards inside the tents. Having established that we were only a few miles from the nearby town of Aveley in Essex a group of us got together, borrowed a hurricane lamp and proceeded to walk into the town. Along our route we passed by an air raid warden who called out to us to extinguish the lamp but hastily took off when he received the caustic reply 'To get stuffed'.

Arriving in Aveley, we soon found a local public house, and the surprise on the landlord's face as we entered his establishment was something to be seen. His greeting to us was to buy us the first round of drinks and to comment that he had never seen anyone look for a pub with an oil lamp. It also caused some concern when it was discovered that we only had a small amount of English currency but plenty of Belgian francs, however, with the assistance from some of the locals we managed a few pints. Although to be fair when they first looked at us it must have been difficult for them to realise that we were members of HM Forces Overseas, looking unwashed, unshaven and in an assortment of uniforms.

After leaving the pub at closing time, complete with hurricane lamp and slightly merry, we endeavoured to find our way back to the army camp. Eventually we entered a field where some soldiers in battle order were being assembled ready to embark for the Continent. As we attempted to pass the soldiers, we found ourselves mixed up amongst them and bawled at by an regimental sergeant major and an officer, who shouted, 'Clear off you rabble'.

When Mac and I found our tent we just lay down on the boards and drifted into sleep, waking some hours later, feeling wet, dirty and very hungry.

The next morning the army provided us with a meagre cold breakfast, and we climbed into our trucks. Nobody had any idea which direction we were heading for, but at least we were on the move.

Somewhere along the route our truck sneezed and came to a halt and looking around I discovered we were in Chigwell in Essex. At the same time, I saw a baker's van and jumping down from the truck, I gave the baker's roundsman all the English money I possessed for a large fruit cake. Considering how hungry we all were, after cutting the cake into twenty slices at least our hunger pains were eased for a short while.

Our French driver having managed to start the truck and our journey continued, passing through London on our way westwards. It was as we drove through the market town of High Wycombe in Buckinghamshire that I caught sight of my mother walking along the High Street but although all of us tried to attract her attention, I had to be content with watching her vanishing figure as our truck turned a corner and she was out of sight.

We by-passed Oxford and some few miles later our convoy entered the confines of RAF Little Rissington, by this time it was about 18.00 hours. Our joy was overwhelming when we discovered that a meal had been prepared for us, however, our joy turned to dismay when we found our meal was a cold salad which comprised mainly of pilchards from a tin. Nevertheless, the hot tea was welcome and we were hungry.

Being a Saturday afternoon in England the camp reminded me of a tennis club with the airmen and WAAFs alike, dressed in their best uniforms obviously finished duty for the weekend. One can only imagine how our intrusion into their neat and clean mess hall was received when they saw this mass of unshaven, dirty and unkempt rabble, dressed like refugees, dismount from the trucks. The permanent staff on the camp couldn't believe their eyes and the NCOs and the station warrant officer almost had a fit when they came to realise that we were also members of the RAF, although not necessarily all British.

Having only one immature young officer, who by this time unfortunately seemed to resemble the rest of us, did not help, but gave us a great delight when the station NCOs who by this time were getting rather dictatorial in their attitude towards us, suddenly discovered that one of us was indeed a commissioned officer, young perhaps, but not prepared to be shouted at.

Within a short time, some order prevailed as the task of feeding us proceeded fairly smoothly, although the permanent airmen and airwomen quickly vacated the mess hall as they saw this horde of non-descript bodies enter the hall. Some two hours later we again re-joined our trucks and headed west again. But just this side of Gloucester our truck had convulsions again and came to a halt. Our predicament wasn't helped by the fact that our driver was a Frenchman whose knowledge of English vehicles was nil and, as the convoy continued, we found ourselves left behind.

Several of the lads had a go at getting the engine started and when eventually they had some success, the Frenchman drove in a manner that left no one in any doubt that the Devil himself was in the cab with the driver.

Towards midnight, Mac pointed out to me some small lights twinkling in the distance and I realised that we were on the outskirts of the very much bombed Welsh town of Swansea. A few miles out of the town and the trucks turned into the entrance of an RAF camp called Fairwood Common. This camp was to be our home for the next eight weeks and was my first introduction to the extremely hospitable Welsh people who not only made us welcome but invited quite a few of us into their homes.

As it was now around 01.00 hours in the morning, I was surprised to find that staff on the camp had prepared for us an excellent hot meal, our first hot food for over forty-eight hours. Following this we were allocated standard wooden billets some distance from the main part of the camp, with approximately thirty men to a billet, although washing and toilet facilities were situated on the main camp.

I clearly remember the sheer luxury of collecting new warmed blankets on that first night and being dropped off at the billets about 02.00 hours. Mac and I secured beds roughly in the centre of the hut and, in a very short time, everyone got their heads down.

The first morning at Fairwood Common proved to be very much a shambles as in the first instance we had been issued with RAF standard issue black pedal cycles to get us to and from the main camp. On this morning we had to get dressed leap onto the bikes and pedal furiously to the toilet blocks trying to arrive before anyone else so as to avoid the crush. Secondly, no one seemed to know what to do with us again and our style of dress caused some consternation to the permanent members of the camp.

Mac and I found that by crossing a section of the perimeter track we were on a main road running alongside the camp. It was then that Mac discovered a pub on the opposite side of the road. Upon entering the pub, the landlord appeared somewhat surprised by our appearance – he couldn't believe that we were members of the RAF. His first reaction was that both of us were escaped German PoWs, although one could not blame him, as Mac was wearing a German Africa Corps hat with an Iron Cross pinned to the front of it.

However, once we established to the landlord and some early morning locals that we were indeed British, though with Mac's Glaswegian accent it took a little time for them to understand him, we managed to get a few beers. The local beer being in short supply the locals were not keen on strangers, nevertheless Mac and I had a pleasant time in the 'Black Boy' public house on the Killay Road before returning to the camp via the way we had come.

Much to our surprise we had not been missed, indeed some of the lads were upset to think that we had found such a handy pub. After hanging around for a couple of hours, our officer suggested that we call it a day as orders concerning our unit had still not arrived. This prompted a surge of bodies emulating the Tour de France in their haste to return to the billets. The general intention was to visit the metropolis of Swansea, but having very little English money presented a major problem until I discovered a WAAF driver who was going into Swansea and she offered to change all our Belgian francs into English currency.

Strangely, it was only when the WAAF returned with the money was I to realise that she had recognised me and that we had been at the same school in London. I vaguely remember her but suggested that I would take her to Swansea the following week, to which she agreed.

Our next problem was the task of making us presentable, again we were saved by providence in the form of a charming WAAF officer in charge of clothing who managed to kit out more than 170 men in a very short time indeed.

In large and small groups, we entered Swansea, our transport being our own trucks which were borrowed for the evening, strictly unofficial. The men now suitably clothed and, with money in their pockets, soon vanished into an assortment of pubs. Mac and I with about six other lads found a tiny pub called the Builder's Arms in Oxford Street and we were well received by the landlord, who insisted on buying the first round. This proved a wise move on his part as for the rest of our time at Fairwood Common, we made the Builder's Arms our local when we were in Swansea.

During my time in Wales, duty permitting, I would often visit Swansea and a well-known dance hall called the Patti Pavilion, which had adjacent to it a public house called The Cricketers. This also became a favourite haunt and considering that in 1944 the ratio was about ten women to every man a great number of associations began from these two establishments.

After a few days, a squadron of Mustang fighters arrived and life took on a more serious approach. It appeared that this squadron had been badly knocked about while in Belgium and were returned to England to reform and to bring the squadron up to strength again.

While I was at Fairwood Common, I had continued to keep in touch with the armourers on our own 341 FF Squadron which was still based at Duerne, and in this manner I was able to find out how they were existing. As it turned out I had always kept in contact with The Duke (Jimmy Reed) and he told me how very much worse the bombardment of the V-1s and V-2s had become. The Duke said that there were many near misses on the squadron with several ground crews being injured and that the weather was appalling with heavy falls of snow and freezing conditions throughout Belgium and Holland.

I felt at the time that I was very fortunate to be back in the United Kingdom where at least I had decent food, a dry bed and was reasonably safe from attack. Just before Christmas, Mac went home for a few days leave and I was occupied with a girlfriend in Swansea. Therefore, it came as an extreme shock when I received a letter from The Duke in which he described to me the tragic events that had occurred on 20 December 1944. In this letter The Duke told me that 341 Squadron had been hit by a V-2 rocket at about 17.00 hours in the afternoon. Fortunately, the majority of the crews had left the flights and hangars and were just entering the mess hall, leaving only a duty crew and flight officer at the hangar when the rocket exploded on the flight office and demolished most of the buildings close by. The Duke went on to say that everyone turned and ran towards the squadron. I heard later from Ken Griffiths that The Duke was one of the first to arrive at the scene and was attempting to dig for what was left of the crews with his bare hands, his face wet with tears. Apparently, the hole was so enormous that several buses could have been put into the crater and the debris was spread all around. Several ground crews were badly injured, and a number of Spitfires were set on fire by the time the rest of the ground crews arrived to help.

Unfortunately, it was on this occasion that among those from the crews on duty who were killed were two armourers from No. 341 FF Squadron, both very close friends of The Duke, Ken Griffiths and me. They were Walter (Timber) Wood aged 23 and Jimmy Manaton aged 38 years of age. Timber Wood came from Sheffield, whilst Jimmy came from London, both were unmarried.

When I first read The Duke's letter, I did not really comprehend the total significance of where both the armourers were killed. However, later on, I began to realise that the hangar where they had been working and had died was in fact the same hangar where I had felt such a feeling of coldness and premonition of death some weeks previously when I had entered this building to write some letters to my mother.

As it turned out it was only a few days after I had left Duerne that both these lads and other members of the ground crews were killed. I thought at the time it could so easily have been me and after so many years I find it difficult to accept that again fate had decreed otherwise.

Both men with the rest of the ground crews who were killed in this particular attack are buried in the Schoonselhof Military Cemetery in Antwerp and I was deeply moved by their loss.

Mac returned from leave and like me was shocked to hear the news regarding the rocket attack at Duerne and although life at Fairwood Common carried on fairly normally, I felt that many of the men were restless and wanted to return to their own individual squadrons in Belgium.

The way things happened our composite echelon was ordered back to Belgium and we were posted back to our original squadrons. This news caused some problems among some of the men who were very much involved with girlfriends around the camp. However, before the orders could be acted upon, 341 Squadron, my own unit, arrived without warning at Fairwood Common, complete with planes, pilots and ground crews.

When I first caught sight of The Duke, Ken Griffiths, Tomo, Bob Pearson and the rest of the armourers I was shocked by their condition and as Mac and I ran to greet them it was difficult to believe our eyes. They all appeared to be suffering from intense fatigue and their complexions had taken on a grey pallor, which I learnt later was caused by loss of sleep and shock. Around the time of their arrival, we had been enduring severe winter conditions at Fairwood Common but from my discussions with Ken Griffiths, he told me of the conditions that prevailed at Duerne after Mac and I left were much worse. Apart from the Germans stepping up their rocket attacks, heavy snow had fallen, followed by gale force winds which created havoc on the airstrip with regard to maintaining the maximum numbers of Spitfires in operational sorties. Temperatures were well below freezing point during the day and were certainly sub-zero at night. Ken explained that one night when he had begun to write letters home, he found the ink in the bottle had frozen solid.

Many of the lads told me at the time that the conditions were made seemingly worse by the intense cold during December 1944 and January 1945. Combined with the continual lack of sleep, cold food and the day and night rocket attacks, it was no wonder that I had difficulty in recognising faces of many of my friends when I first saw them on arrival at Fairwood Common. As we had one night left before Mac and I returned to Belgium,

I arranged for most of the armourers to meet at the Builder's Arms in Swansea and the evening proved quite a great success, although many of us ended up by walking the 4 or so miles back to camp in the early hours.

The following morning our composite echelon assembled at the main camp for the beginning of our journey back to Europe. A sad affair after such a brief re-union with all the lads from 341 who were staying on for a further two weeks at Fairwood Common.

At Swansea station we joined a special train later that evening and many emotional farewells were said by the different crew members who had become involved with the local girls, including WAAFs from the camp.

The journey to London passed very quickly and arriving at Paddington station around 03.45 hours did nothing to excite the imagination. As we had some three hours to kill Mac and I wandered out into Praed Street and were fortunate to find an all-night café open. Re-joining the lads back at Paddington, we proceeded to Victoria Station and then another train journey to Folkstone where the whole echelon embarked on board a ship and headed towards France once more.

Chapter 10

Back to the Fighting

After a perfect crossing of the Channel we arrived in Calais, so different from our previous crossing from Ostend to Tilbury. Once we had disembarked, the echelon boarded a very long train and soon began our journey through France, Belgium and into Holland arriving at Tilburg where we stayed at an RAF transit camp.

During this time the task of returning the individual crews to their original squadrons began, Mac and I said a fond farewell to many of the friends we had made within the composite echelon before we both were directed to our 145 Wing Headquarters was now stationed at Schjindel a small town near Eindhoven in Holland. We had a tiresome journey arriving at Schjindel late at night and spent two weeks at headquarters until our own No. 341 Squadron arrived back from England. Our squadrons return was indeed a welcome occasion and from somewhere a few bottles of champagne appeared. The first evening back amongst our fellow armourers was spent swapping tales and disposing of the champers.

The town of Schjindel including the airstrip had been for some time the centre of quite a battle. In all, the town had been taken thirteen times by both the German and British infantry. The area was devoid of any trees, only the stumps remained where once a fairly heavily wooded area existed. It was in conversation with some ground crews from another squadron on an advanced airstrip nearby that I was told of them finding German dead still lying around unburied, in and around the dispersal points of the airstrip.

Fortunately, we only remained at Schjindel for about another ten days, but the mixture was as before, early morning sorties and hectic activity until about 19.00 hours in the evening. We suffered losses of planes and pilots, but our daily life was not subject to the bombardment of rockets that we had experience in Antwerp.

One tragic incident which marred our stay at Schjindel concerned one of our youngest ground crew members. Bob Tyler was a London lad and only eighteen years of age. All the way through France and Belgium he had been an avid collector of souvenirs, German Iron Crosses, helmets etc. While all of us had been warned not to wander away from the airstrip into the adjoining fields because of mines and booby traps Bob Tyler chose to ignore this instruction. He had been looking around a deserted house in a nearby field when he trod on a German mine which had been missed by the mine detectors. I remember the explosion and saw the black pall of smoke mushrooming skywards. It was Bob Tyler's last war souvenir. He lost a leg and was lucky to escape with his life.

Leaving Schjindel in the now familiar two section move, I was joined in the advance ground crew by Ken Griffiths, whilst Mac remained behind. Our destination this time was Germany and I wondered what our reception would be like once we crossed the Rhine.

Making the normal early start we left Schjindel, the convoy winding its way through villages and towns. Bypassing some of the larger towns I began to see the devastation of the towns in an around the Dutch-German border. Passing into the open countryside the number of bomb craters were enormous, everywhere I looked there appeared to be complete chaos and entering into Germany most towns we passed seemed to be devoid of human habitation. As for the German civilians it was retribution indeed to be a witness to the damage inflicted by the Allied bombers. In towns like Emmerich and Cleve the picture was the same with the ever-present feeling of death everywhere.

Some few miles inside the German border our truck coughed and came to a halt. Ken and I climbed down from the vehicle, as we looked around, we appeared to be in a desert of bomb craters, large and small. The truck having been repaired, we continued our journey; our ultimate destination was a village called Drope a few kilometres from Lingen but because of the breakdown we were several hours behind our main convoy and forced to park alongside the Dortmund-Elms canal quite near to an Army camp.

Among the crew in our truck, we had one lad who could find anything, anytime, anywhere and because of our delay, we had run out of food. Somewhere about midnight this lad vanished from the truck and re-appeared some minutes later with a large dixie of hot tea. It seemed that the army lads had been brewing up and had left it unattended. Later on, we were paid a visit by the irate soldiers who made unpleasant threats as to what they would do to whoever had stolen their tea, however, we must have looked the picture of innocence because they wandered off still seeking the culprit who had robbed them.

The next morning, we moved off and soon arrived at Drope, the area was one vast stretch of fields converted into an airstrip which contained several wings and already occupied by a number of Typhoon squadrons.

It was now the beginning of April 1945 and, the weather being good, a massive number of airstrikes were flown each day and as on our previous airstrips we had losses of planes and pilots. The fact that it was apparent to all that the war in Germany was coming to a climax seemed to encourage everyone from pilots to ground crews to get the Spitfires re-armed and re-bombed quicker than ever and increase the number of air strikes on the German towns.

My time at Drope, near Lingen was marked by three events, the first was an accident which could have ended my life, the second was the celebration of my 21st birthday and the third was another escape from serious injury and possibly death on the day the war ended in Europe.

The accident occurred one day when I was sat astride the top of our flight marquee which was used as our squadron headquarters. I was in the process of replacing the camouflage patches on the exterior of the marquee when Mac, for some unknown reason, decided to clean his rifle. One moment I was on top of the marquee and the next I was laid on the ground, swearing like a trooper.

Apparently, Mac, after cleaning his rifle, held up the gun in a firing position and had taken aim in my direction and pulled the trigger. To his surprise a bullet was fired from the rifle and made a hole just between my legs on its trajectory skywards. Mac had overlooked the fact that a bullet was in the breach of the rifle when he took aim and fired.

Needless to say he was very shocked by what he had done and seeing me lying on the ground, he feared the worst. However, hearing my tirade of abuse directed at him, he quickly realised that I was unhurt. Ken Griffiths came to my aid and helped me to my feet and for some minutes panic took over because, without knowing the cause of the excitement, everyone assumed the airstrip was under attack by the Germans and that a sniper had fired at me.

Fortunately, nothing more was heard of the incident. Nevertheless I was always very cautious and wary of anybody holding a rifle for whatever reason.

The second event was on 26 April 1945, my birthday, it proved to be a beautiful sunny day and for the first time I began to appreciate the countryside around us. Everything seemed alive with colour and for a brief moment of stillness I could hear some birds singing in the nearby trees, abruptly brought to an early end by the roar of our squadron Spitfires returning once more from another sortie. It seemed quite odd to me at the time that amongst all the fighting and the killing involved with the war that I had never really appreciated the scenery which surrounded me, before reality again once more took over.

I had during the day acquired a couple of dozen bottles of beer, so my health was drunk but I felt at the time, it was rather an anti-climax as I had always hoped to have celebrated my twenty-first birthday in England with my family.

Following my birthday, many rumours were rife concerning the end of the war in Italy, however, nothing official was announced so our squadron sorties carried on daily.

It was in the first days of May that we were told that the German forces in the Italian campaign had surrendered. The weather was extremely good, so our squadrons were operating far into German airspace, when suddenly the news was flashed to the squadron that the German forces had capitulated. At first the ground crews did not believe it but when told officially by our CO that the war in Europe was over, the ground crew felt as if they were in a vacuum after the endless days and nights of intense activity. It was 8 May 1945.

Strange as it may seem there did not appear to be any urgency anymore, but the French pilots took the news in their stride. One group collected all the wooded jet tanks from under the fuselages of the Spitfires and piled them in a heap. A pilot fired his revolver into the centre of the tanks and an enormous flame shot skywards as the petrol in the tanks exploded whilst other pilots charged about the airstrip firing their revolvers into the air.

It was whilst the ground crews were witnessing the release of all the pent-up emotions and tensions that Mac and I drove away from the airstrip in one of our Bedford trucks to anywhere which offered safety while the lunatics tired themselves out.

Driving along the main road for some miles passing burnt out Tiger tanks and the general debris of war, Mac turned off and drove down a very narrow lane until we entered a very heavily wooded area when suddenly I said to Mac stop: 'I've had enough let's go back.' As the truck came to a halt, I jumped down from the truck and too my horror I saw that the front wheels of the truck were only a few feet from the edge of a sheer drop of some 80 or so feet. On closer inspection I discovered that there had been a bridge spanning a small ravine which the Germans in their retreat had blown up but because of a bend in the road and the overhanging trees and foliage we had failed to see.

Mac's face turned a milky white and I felt cold and began to shake all over and it seemed a long time before either of us could think about returning to the airstrip. On our return journey Mac and I said very little to each other but I have never forgotten the place or the date. I felt then as I do now, that it just wasn't meant to be. Someone, somewhere, had decreed it was not going to happen there.

Driving into the airstrip we saw that the fires were still burning all over the place and re-joining the rest of the armourers, someone handed me a bottle of beer and it appeared that a party was in progress.

Later on, that evening, several radios were tuned into London and as the announcer took the listeners around the main cities in Great Britain we could hear the celebrations going on and a certain sadness came over the crews, combined with a quietness which seemed to settle over the whole airstrip. Most of the crews not on duty began to write letters home, or just lay on their beds smoking but looking into nowhere. I thought, like me perhaps, they were thinking of absent friends and all we had been through together. Even the birds were quiet that evening.

The following day, 9 May, was a bright day, and everyone appeared very happy, the tensions of the previous day seemed to have evaporated. An inter-squadron football match was organised and proved a great success, although not for me, as I played in goal and let in seven goals, before the game ended.

After lunch an unfortunate fatal accident occurred to a young English pilot who had recently joined No. 345 Squadron from England. The pilot had never flown any operational sorties and to familiarize himself with the Spitfire, he had taken off and was doing a low flying exercise over the airstrip.

I was sitting outside our tent with Ken Griffiths, Mac, The Duke and Bob Pearson when I saw the Spitfire go into a slow dive, I recall saying to the others at the time, 'That Spit's too low' and as we all stood up to get a better view the plane seemed to glide straight into the ground, a muffled explosion followed and a great black mushroom of smoke spiralled skywards with the crackle of flames as the plane became engulfed in a blazing inferno.

Everybody ran towards the plane, but the rescue of the pilot was impossible, as the ammunition onboard began exploding and the flames drove the rescuers and crash teams back from the intense heat.

Later that day a fellow pilot told us that the pilot of the crashed Spitfire had been married just before being posted out to Germany, and No. 345 Squadron. That evening it was again very quiet on the airstrip and it had started to rain, the droplets running down the sides of the tents, forming little streams of water as they joined up with the water running from the other tents. Not a happy end to the first day of peace, 9 May 1945.

Life took on a rather mundane appearance as inspections became the order of the day, but things improved when, towards the end of June, orders were received for the wing to move up to a German brick-built airfield at Fassberg, a few miles from Celle, near Hanover.

Our information was that this was a first-class airfield with brick billets and all the facilities that went with it. Again, Ken Griffiths and I were in the advanced party leaving Lingen at the ungodly hour of 04.00 hours.

The convoy that left Lingen was quite a sight mainly because many of the lads had acquired chassis on which box like caravans had proved to be extremely comfortable. It was then only natural that the owners of the caravans, who were in the advanced section, should wish to shackle them to the rear of the trucks that they would be riding in.

As the convoy of vehicles headed onto the main road, led by a lonely despatch rider, I began to imagine that I was in another world, as in the half light of dawn I saw some trucks shrouded completely in darkness, while other vehicles were reflecting the slim pencil line of the dawn light as it began to widen against the black sky of the previous night. Looking out from the rear of the truck I felt a chilling feeling as we headed further into Germany.

Chapter 11

Fassberg

After travelling for some miles across Germany, the convoy was giving the appearance of an endless stream of dustcarts, rather than the advance section of a fighter wing. As the trucks rattled through the German towns, one by one the home-built caravans were beginning to disintegrate and depositing their personal effects onto the road as the wooden sides of the caravans collapsed.

Moving through one German town a caravan literally fell apart as the truck towing it sped round a corner in the road. I was witness to the ludicrous sight of the owner endeavouring to pick up his kit plus all the personal belongings which were spread half on the pavement and the other half in the road. The scene was like a music hall sketch as the lad involved tried hard to collect his bits and pieces. His task was not helped by the chorus of catcalls and ribald comments which came from the direction of a large block of flats nearby, the balconies which were filled with German women who were enjoying the embarrassing situation to the full.

Eventually all the caravans had to be dispensed with and were abandoned by the side of the road, such was their pathetic end with their owner's kit being hurled into any nearby truck.

The day began rather hot, the journey was beginning to take its toll as we passed several small German towns and villages but although our thirst grew worse the orders were to keep moving.

The convoy of trucks rumbled on until we reached the outskirts of Hanover, and I realised what a beautiful city it had once been. Although the large number of air raids by Allied bombers had caused untold damage which was evident for all to see. After several detours our convoy reached Fassberg.

The gates to the airfield were wide open and the sight which presented itself to the ground crews weary from travelling through Germany was indeed tremendous. Large gardens appeared alongside the clean road into the main part of the camp which contained substantial brick billets. Nothing seemed to be damaged in anyway, not even a broken window in any of the buildings. After alighting from the truck, Ken Griffiths and I saw that the whole area was completely surrounded by a large number of tall trees with German fighters and bombers parked near the runways, but apart from slight damage, the planes appeared not to have been touched.

Investigating the crew's billets, we discovered that each room on three storeys contained metal beds, even German helmets and other equipment obviously left behind as the previous occupants left in a hurry.

At either end of each floor were sumptuous toilets, showers and washing facilities, plus amongst all things we had electricity. Both Ken and I stripped off and leapt into the showers. Some ground crews couldn't wait and they just went into the showers fully clothed; such was their delight at the facilities available.

After the showers Ken and I wandered into the nearby woodlands and were amazed to discover a complete skittle alley perfectly intact, also adjacent was a store containing new German Luftwaffe uniforms in abundance.

Some of the ground crews had come upon a BMW motorcycle and some eight or nine lads were balanced on top of each other as they roared along the perimeter of the airfield before ending up spreadeagled on the grass verge as they over balanced.

Having secured a room on the first floor for Ken and me, with beds for The Duke and Bob Pearson, it wasn't very long before the second section of our wing arrived at Fassberg.

Adjacent to the camp but set within the heavy woodlands were many houses and chalets. These homes were originally used by members of the Luftwaffe and their families and when the men were captured their wives and girlfriends were left behind. Quite naturally these women were seeking work and soon many of them took on the role of cooks, cleaners, etc., to the different squadrons based at the camp. It was also understandable that many friendships and associations began between the ground crews and the women employed on the airfield. The ratio of men to women was approximately one man to five women, so night operations began immediately although the ban on fraternisation between Germans and British servicemen was still in force.

The non-fraternisation ban proved to be rather a farce, because as soon as darkness covered the land, the secretive exits of many ground crews was very evident as they left the billets and make their way to the respective homes of their German girlfriends' homes set in the woods.

On one such occasion Ken Griffiths and I were on duty one night and as we were returning to our billets about 05.00 hours in the morning, we were astounded to see the mass of men who came out from the woods, heading for the billets on the camp. I said to Ken at the time, it reminded me of a crowd leaving a football match. This situation continued for a few weeks before the powers that be decreed that the non-fraternisation ban should be lifted but by this time this order had become just a rubber stamp, as the men's night operations were in full swing and nobody bothered about the ban.

Whilst the squadrons were at Fassberg, some flying was taking place and we were still servicing the Spitfires, although the ground crews in general felt that they were just killing time, while the great Allied war machine was being put into reverse.

Organised games and student courses were set up to help to prepare the men for their return to civilian life. Regimentation took over, complete with drill parades and peace time discipline. Insignificant NCOs arrived fresh from England and strutted about the camp like bantam cocks, the ground crews called them the 'Gestapo'.

On the camp we had an excellent canteen and bar and as the older members of our squadrons' ground crews were being sent home to England for demobilization there were a series of farewell parties and we had many happy evenings, although at the end of each evening a touch of sadness came over us all.

At first it wasn't noticed but as the weeks went on our group of armourers was slowly growing smaller in number. As each left Fassberg there was a certain amount of bravado but underneath many farewells there was a great deal of emotion particularly between men who had been together for a long time. In some cases, armourers like Ken Griffiths and Jimmy Reed had been close friends for some four years. There was always talk of a big re-union one day but nobody really believed it would happen.

It was during the early part of August 1945 that I was injured after falling from the wing of a Spitfire. I was checking the guns of the plane and had turned to face the rear of the plane when my feet slipped on some oil on the wing and I fell awkwardly, landing in a heap on the concrete runway underneath the plane. On attempting to rise to my feet, I felt a searing pain in my right leg and promptly fell to the ground again. Ken, seeing me fall from the plane and in agony, called some of the lads who carried me like a sack of potatoes to the camp hospital.

I spent that night in the hospital and the next morning I was transferred to a civilian hospital at Celle where orthopaedic specialists prodded and pulled my leg about. When they had finished their examination, it was decided to give my leg intensive massage treatment and following this I was slowly able to begin to walk again.

On returning to Fassberg, I found quite a few more of our ground crews had returned to England and in their place were some new recruits fresh from training school.

Following my return, I had my first and only encounter with the Hitler Youth. Some twenty of them had been told to report to me to carry out some cleaning duties in the crews' billets. When they eventually arrived, I soon became aware of their arrogance and hatred of anything British. One of their group, who seemed to be their leader and spoke English fluently, told me in no uncertain terms that they did not intend to carry out any cleaning for the British bastards. As I began to walk towards them, I realised that some of them were only about twelve to fifteen years of age. After informing the leader that they had better get on with the job all I achieved was a very sullen and insolent attitude, plus a few well-known hand gestures. Not caring too much for Germans of any age, I came to the conclusion that this lot were attempting to intimidate me and by this time were almost achieving it.

However, feeling that the end justified the means, I walked into the crew room picked up a rifle and promptly put one up the spout with a great deal of expertise. Whereupon the Hitler Youth all came to attention, the leader saluted me and from that moment I had no more trouble from the inheritors of the Third Reich.

A few days later my leg began to swell up and back to hospital I went. Further examinations followed and then the doctors decided to send me to a rehabilitation centre at Blankenberge on the Belgian coast.

I again returned to Fassberg just to collect some kit and say a brief farewell to Ken, Mac, Bob and The Duke, before being transported to Hanover station and put on board a train for Brussels in Belgium.

After a tiring journey I arrived at Brussels and had a twenty-minute wait before boarding another train en route to Blankenberge.

Chapter 12

Simone at Blankenberge

The rehabilitation centre at Blankenberge was situated in two large hotels facing the sea, one was named Excelsior, whilst the other was aptly named the Continental. I was allocated a room on the fifth floor of the latter. After depositing my kit in the room, I reported to the medical officer in charge of the centre, who gave me a minor inspection and advised me that I should give my leg as much exercise as possible and to be in bed by 22.00 hours each night whilst I remained at the centre and that I was free until 09.00 hours the following morning.

There were about twenty or so patients of varying nationalities who arrived with me that day and I soon discovered I was to share a room with a French-Canadian serving with the Canadian Air Force. His name was Jimmy and from the very beginning I nicknamed him 'Frenchy' as his surname was impossible to pronounce.

Most of the lads who arrived that day were walking cases, so after sorting out our personal belongings, Frenchy and I had a meal together. During our conversation, Frenchy explained that he was serving with a Canadian squadron of Spitfires, strangely enough his squadron was only some 3 miles from my own squadron stationed at Fassberg.

Frenchy's hometown was Montreal and he was 100 per cent a Frenchman. When he discovered that I was serving with the

French Lorraine and Alsace squadrons and that I had strong connections with Canada, via my eldest brother who was a Canadian and lived in Hamilton, Ontario, we hit it off very well right from the start.

From his conversation Frenchy had decided that he had seen enough of the war and now it was over, he wanted to return to Montreal. Not having any success through normal channels, Frenchy had taken the law into his own hands, so to speak. He had used his own ·5 Colt automatic and shot a hole the size of a ten pence piece through the centre of his left hand. An extreme measure I thought at the time but after spending some six weeks with this character, I learnt a great deal about determination from Frenchy.

The hole in his left hand was quite a mess as the bullet passed completely through the centre of the hand, severing some ligaments. Fortunately for Frenchy, the doctors had saved his hand although he had lost some of the feeling in his fingers.

My relationship with this French-Canadian was to begin a phase in my life that holds a very special place in my heart even until the time of writing, as the reader will come to understand later.

Having covered a lot of ground in a very short time, Frenchy and I decided to see what life we could find in our new surroundings in Blankenberge. I had been told by one of the staff at the centre that some 300 yards from the hotel the Belgian Red Cross had taken over a pre-war casino and had organised it into a servicemen's club, called the 21 Club.

As it was now around 20.30 hours in the evening, we decided to investigate this nearby club situated just along the promenade and facing the sea. Upon entering this establishment, I soon discovered that it was an extremely well-run organisation with many facilities for servicemen. It was staffed entirely by young and very pretty Belgian girls, who were all strictly vetted by the local Red Cross and Catholic Association, before being allowed to work at the 21 Club.

Being a Sunday evening, the club was packed with all branches of the services and many different nationalities were fully represented. On entering the spacious bar area, Frenchy ordered two beers and a bottle of cognac and, as we sat down at a nearby table, it soon became clear to me that Frenchy enjoyed the opposite sex, as he was continually speaking fluent French in chatting up the many Belgian waitresses who passed back and forth by our table with their trays of drinks.

We had been in the club some minutes before I realised that a dance was in progress in the large ballroom adjacent to the bar and as the music ceased for the interval, the bar began to fill up with thirsty dancers. Frenchy was by this time getting the flavour of the place and the more cognac he consumed the more affable he became.

Early on in the evening Frenchy had told me how he hated anything that was British and I was surprised by his attitude towards me, as indeed I was very much British, nevertheless our friendship began to ripen from the first night at the 21 Club.

As the interval came to an end the orchestra began to start up again in the ballroom, Frenchy caught the eye of a Belgian girl standing near the bar, she was fairly tall and well built. She had obviously been watching him for some minutes and when he spoke to her in French, she crossed to our table and sat down. She said her name was Janine and told us that her friend who was standing with the other waitresses at the bar was called Simone.

Janine called for Simone to join us and introduced me to her, she explained that they both worked at the club but as Sunday was their day off, they had obtained permission to attend that evening's dance.

Frenchy and Janine were conversing in French, and I tried out my limited French on Simone who surprised me by speaking in perfect English. She told me that she was just seventeen and lived in Bruges and that her family were very strict Catholics.

Whilst Simone was talking to me, I noticed how petite she was and with her dark black hair and her eyes which always seemed to be smiling, I felt quite disturbed by her presence.

As the dance was now ending, I suggested that Frenchy and I should accompany the two girls home to Bruges but soon discovered that the local Red Cross always organised the Belgian girls' transport to their respective homes. It was then that I suggested to Simone that we should meet the following afternoon, to my surprise she agreed and said she would meet me at 16.00 hours on the pier the next day.

On the following day Frenchy and I presented ourselves to the medical officer who viewed us with a certain distaste and after examining us suggested that we should take more water with it.

After lunch Frenchy and I walked along the pier and had only just reached the café at the end of the pier when Janine and Simone appeared. Both Frenchy and Janine decided to walk into town whilst Simone and I went into the café where a tea dance was in progress. After a little while we came out of the café and sat on the very end of the pier. I recall Simone telling me how difficult it had been to meet me due to the strictness of her parents and that she had been training to be a ballet dancer but an injury to her ankle had put paid to her hopes regarding that career.

Having a camera with me I took some photographs of Simone with her back towards the sea, at the time she appeared very shy, which still shows even today as I look at the photographs I took of her some thirty-five years on.

We had spent most of the afternoon on the pier just sitting and talking together and the time just seemed to fly and, as Simone was on duty at the 21 Club that evening, I walked with her to the entrance, just in time to meet Frenchy and Janine.

Having arranged to meet the two girls later on, Frenchy and I returned to our hotel. As we were having a meal together, I mentioned to Frenchy that I felt that I was becoming infatuated with Simone. I recall Frenchy gave me a quizzical look and just said, '*Ce la fayr rien*'. Later on in the same year I was to realise what an impact Simone was to make on me, or for that matter the consequences which were to follow our six-week relationship, continuing even until the time of writing this book.

Later that evening when Frenchy and I were at the 21 Club, quite a number of servicemen appeared to be having a party to which Frenchy joined and did a routine of attempting to stand on his head on top of the table, eventually overbalancing and ending up on the floor, much to the enjoyment of the onlookers.

By the time the two girls had finished work at the club, I was feeling a little heady and Simone was hanging on to me like grim death. She suggested that we go along to a small café adjoining the club for some coffee. After leaving the club I felt less like coffee and we just walked along the promenade until my head began to clear. Finding a seat, we both sat down and I sensed that the chemistry between us was electric. It was on hearing the church clock chime 01.00 hours that we both realised that Simone had missed the Red Cross transport back to Bruges, also Simone was concerned what her parents would have to say. After wandering around Blankenberge for a little while, I was very fortunate to meet an Army truck which was heading towards Bruges and gave us a lift into the town, eventually arriving at her home around 02.30 hours in the morning. It was only after Simone had entered her home was I suddenly aware of my own predicament. I was in the centre of Bruges without any hope of finding transport back to Blankenberge.

Fearing the worst, I began to walk along the road towards the coast, but it wasn't long before my leg began to ache. Having completed about a mile I reached a road junction where there was a low wall. Deciding to take a rest, I had just sat down when I saw some headlamps in the distance which proved to be a large Army truck. Fortunately the driver saw me and in a very short time I was back outside the hotel in Blankenberge. It was only when I alighted from the truck did I discover that I had been sitting on boxes of explosives – apparently the authorities considered it safer to transport these dangerous boxes at night.

The next morning at breakfast I explained to Frenchy about my trip to Bruges and seeing Simone home, to which he replied, 'You are mad'. Later that morning I went through the same routine with the medical officer and was able to receive some heat massage for my leg.

Shortly after lunch I made my way along to the pier and to my surprise Simone was waiting for me. She explained it had been difficult but explained to her parents that the Red Cross bus had left early the previous night.

It was such a beautiful day that Simone suggested we go for a swim and for the rest of the afternoon we spent our time in the sea and on the beach. As the sun began to set, I realised how hungry I was, and Simone and I made our way to a café called Francais which was owned by friends of Simone's family. The owner and his wife Pieter and Yvette seeing our plight allowed us to wash and change in one of their first-floor bedrooms. It proved to be the longest changing session ever, but Pieter and Yvette proved to be very understanding friends to both Simone and me during my stay at Blankenberge.

These afternoon meetings with Simone became the routine whilst I remained at the rehabilitation centre. I would meet Simone about lunchtime after I had spent the morning receiving treatment for my leg and take the opportunity to swim in the afternoons with her. Then in the evenings we would meet again when she was on duty at the 21 Club.

One afternoon Simone asked me about my family in England and had the war changed me. I told her that I hated the killing and the endless days and nights trying to survive. I said that the loss of personal friends affected me so much that each death seemed to take a piece of me with it, also how scared I had been in the event of being injured or maimed for life. I wasn't afraid of total death but dreaded the thought of being paralysed or completely incapacitated for life.

Simone had given me the nickname of Simmy and many times when we were alone, she would ask me when I had to return to Germany would I come back for her. I knew she was in love with me and I with her and given the opportunity I would have married Simone but I also knew of her family's resistance to her association with me.

With hindsight, perhaps I lacked the courage of my convictions but nevertheless it was a decision that for me ended in tragedy the following year.

I was aware that my six weeks stay at Blankenberge was coming to an end, but it still came as a shock to receive my official orders to report to my squadron at Fassberg in Germany. It was now the middle of October and the atmosphere was decidedly taking on a wintery look about it, so different from the beginning of September when I met Simone for the first time.

I received my orders on the Wednesday with instructions to begin my journey back to Fassberg the next morning Thursday at 08.00 hours from the station at Blankenberge.

Having only one more night in Blankenberge, I felt somewhat at a loss when I met Simone as normal on the pier at lunchtime, she had thought it would go on forever and was quite upset by my news.

Later that evening in the 21 Club when I was saying goodbye to Frenchy and the other friends I had made in the club, I knew that I would never meet Frenchy again and his friendship was something I still remember with affection many years after.

As the evening was now coming to an end the chaperon of the girls at the club allowed Simone and Janine to join our small group who were waiting to leave the club and as the orchestra played the last song, I realised it was called 'Fascination' a very apt name for my relationship with Simone.

It was just after midnight when Simone and I walked away from the club and headed in the direction of the pier, to us it was a symbol of our first meeting. Standing on the pier I looked out towards the sea and wondered what fate had in store for us both. The war in Europe was over but England and my home seemed a million miles away on the pier at Blankenberge that night.

Leaving the pier, we both walked towards Pieter and Yvette's café in the town. I was by this time concerned for Simone as she had obviously missed the transport back to Bruges, however, on this occasion Yvette offered us accommodation at the café which we gratefully accepted.

The room faced the sea and I listened for some time to the sounds that only came from the stillness of the night with the waves washing over the sands on the beach. Many things Simone and I talked about, those few hours we had together that last night, as we tried to plan our future when I returned once I was finished with the Air Force. I knew I really loved this Belgian girl and she in return loved me.

Just after 07.00 hours Yvette brought us some coffee and shortly after this I walked with Simone to the station and finding the correct platform, we entered an empty compartment of the waiting train. I remember hearing the church clock strike the half hour and I knew it was time to go. Simone stood on the platform as the train pulled out and I leaned out of the carriage window watching her until she became a blurred image that blended in with the rest of the scenery. This was the last time I saw Simone, as I headed back towards Germany.

Chapter 13

Back to the Squadron

After a long and tiring journey by rail only interrupted by the changing of engines and train crews at each border crossing on my way back to Fassberg, I arrived many hours later on the camp and upon entering my billet I found the building was deserted. I was told by one of the lads that The Duke, Ken Griffiths and Bob Pearson were in Hanover on a short course apart from that everyone around appeared to be strangers.

Reporting to the station medical officer I was given a quick medical check and advised to take things easy for a few days. On wandering down onto the squadron I met up with some of my original ground crews who were pleased to see me back and they told me that several members of the squadron had been posted back to England, while others had been sent to other squadrons on different airstrips in Germany.

Upon returning to the billet, I found that The Duke, Ken and Bob had returned from Hanover; they told me all the past and present gossip, whilst I told them about my six weeks at Blankenberge. I mentioned to Ken about Simone and that I wanted to marry her, to which Ken replied, 'Don't waste time talking about it, do it'.

The next two weeks passed and life at Fassberg became very tedious. The lads were agitating to get home and for most of us the peacetime existence in Germany did little to excite the imagination. Somehow it seemed as if there wasn't any purpose anymore, just routine exercises both for pilots and ground crews. As friendships blossomed between the British servicemen and the German girls, to me it appeared too soon to forget what we had all been through, but I also thought that's life and it goes on whatever the consequences.

It was towards the end of November 1945 that my right leg finally collapsed, and I found myself once again in hospital, this time it was Celle near Hanover. After further intensive investigation by a number of doctors, it was decided to send me back to England to have an operation on my right leg. I had time only to just say goodbye to the lads before I found myself on board a Dakota aircraft with many other lads suffering from various injuries en route to England.

Some of the lads onboard were stretcher cases and required constant attention throughout our flight home by the nurses who were absolutely marvellous. After talking to one of the lads on a stretcher, I felt very inadequate when I considered my own injury.

As I was able to sit up, I could look out of the windows in the aircraft, it was only then that I began to realise the amount of devastation which the Allied and American bombers had inflicted on the German towns and countryside. The whole area we were flying over was pock marked with bomb craters and large areas of various towns were just heaps of rubble, retribution indeed I thought as I looked down upon Hitler's Germany.

Crossing over the centre of Cologne, I was surprised to see the cathedral standing almost untouched but everything around it was smashed to the ground. As the aircraft left the German air space on through Holland and into Belgium, I thought of the lads left back at Fassberg and of how many were left from the original ground crews who landed in France the previous year. I thought of the days and nights we had all spent living like nomadic tribesmen as we travelled through France into Belgium, Holland and then onto Germany.

Many faces seemed to pass through my mind as I sat in the Dakota winding its way back to England. A large number of men, both pilots and ground crews, had been killed over the past year. The place which will always be remembered with affection by those of us who survived is Wevelgem in Belgium but the town which still gives me a cold shudder whenever the name is mentioned is Duerne near Antwerp and I know I am not alone in this feeling. To those ground crews and pilots who were stationed at the hell hole during December 1944 through to January 1945 and are still alive, they were indeed very fortunate men. As one member of our squadron said only a few months ago, every day since we left Duerne is a bonus.

Leaving the Belgian coastline, I could see Blankenberge and the city of Bruges in the distance and I thought about Simone and wondered what she was doing. I had written to her from Germany but had received no reply, although with my movements my mail still had not caught up with me.

The English coastline soon appeared and then across the English countryside until we reached Lyneham in Wiltshire where the Dakota landed. Ambulances soon ferried us to the nearby hospital, where we received a hot meal and a chance to clean up before being put into beautiful warm beds with clean white sheets.

Later on, we were each given a bottle of Guinness, and this topped up with some Champagne from one of the lads with us, the last thing I remember was consuming about half a pint, before oblivion took over. Welcome back to England.

Per ardua ad astra.

When Germany surrendered on 8 May 1945, I sat with so many other young men on an airfield in the heart of Hitler's Germany, listening to a radio announcer reporting the excitement and the joy of the people back home that the war was over. We all felt on that particular airfield, that we were in a stage play that had come to an end. One cannot describe in words, the silence that surrounded not only the area we were in but the silence between us young men.

Islington was a long way from the middle of Germany that historic night, but I was very grateful to be alive and come safely through the war. I was just twenty-one, having celebrated my twenty-first birthday two weeks earlier. I asked myself at that time a question: 'What was a boy from Islington doing here?'.

I have never returned to Germany. My home at 162 Barnsbury Road, next door to the Eclipse public house, no longer exits as I knew it. It came through the war unscathed, however, in the late 1970s the house was demolished and rebuilt in a slightly more modern style of a three-storey house, minus the shop it the front and with no visible evidence of the airey or cellar which led to the downstairs living room and scullery, where so much of my early young days were fashioned.

On one of my more recent visits to Barnsbury Road in 1984, I entered the Eclipse for a lunch time drink and noticed that the pub had also been altered and modernised inside. When I left the establishment an hour or so later, I stood in the road outside. Perhaps it was nostalgia or an old man's dream but for a brief moment I had a vision of my family and school friends, just the way we were, way back in the dark ages of the 1930s. Suddenly, broken off by the reality and noise of a large civilian airliner passing overhead on its way to Heathrow Airport. Barnsbury Road still exists for me, sadly the past has gone like an hourglass empty of sand.

A little later that day, I was in conversation with a gentleman who was living a little way along the road, about the history of the neighbourhood. He told me he was from South Africa and worked in the City of London. Before we parted, he pointed to the open spaces opposite his house on the other side of Barnsbury Road, including Pulteney Street, and asked what had stood on this open grassed area. I explained to him about the land mine and bombs which had destroyed the houses and families during the Blitz, and ended by saying that it was for me a monument to a great many friends. At that time, I told this gentleman that it was my sincere intent to write a story about the Islington I knew in the 1930s and 1940s. Perhaps in due time this gentleman may have the opportunity of reading my story and begin to understand what Islington was really like during that period, and why it holds for many people, no longer living in the area, a special place in their memories.

To have been a boy in Islington left you with an indelible stamp for the rest of your life. It has been impossible for me to include all the names of people I knew in the district, not because I do not recall their names, but because I could go on forever. I can only trust that those unwittingly omitted from this story will understand.

Both my parents and my brothers and sister have all died over the years leaving me the youngest of our family, the only survivor from this generation. However, at the insistence and coercion of my sons and daughters I felt this tale needed to be told. Over the years from before the turn of the century into the present day, Islington has and its ups and downs, from beautiful Georgian and Victorian houses in the 1800s with families living in the houses enjoying the advantages of both servants and carriages, to the period when the owners and landlords of these houses were grateful to let out their properties to the less well off. Thus, large four storey houses became tenements, teaming with young children and the poverty that existed before the First World War, right through until the beginning of the Second World War.

In the early 1960s, Islington began to take on its former image and its local population has changed dramatically compared to when the area was filled with families between the wars. In still have many friends who, with their families, still live in Islington, and I am sure they will appreciate my sentiments that, despite all I have seen and done, I am still, at heart, a boy from Islington.

In conclusion may I inform the reader that in November 1979, whilst I was researching the book, I wrote to the well-known comedian Mr Michael Bentine to establish certain facts which were connected with the Belgian 350 Squadron commanded by Commandant Donnet with whom Mr Bentine was attached during the war.

In return Mr Bentine's reply to me was very helpful and concluded with wishes for my success with the book and included a few sincere words of a personal nature, which Mr Bentine has given me his permission to reproduce and include at the end of my story. I believe the content is self-explanatory.

'I sometimes look around now and wonder what we were fighting for, and if it was all worth it!'

Yours sincerely
Michael Bentine

Appendix

Lost Companions

Copy of letter received by the author from Mrs Helen Archibald of Edinburgh, February 1980.

I read in the *Edinburgh Evening News* that you are writing a book about the Free French Squadrons stationed at Turnhouse during the war.

My late husband served with them as an armourer, he thought they were a grand bunch of men; he often spoke of them after the war.

We were on holiday in Blackpool when my late husband saw one of his pilots on the television, he was now holding a post within the French Government. During the time the French Squadrons were at Turnhouse, my husband had a nasty experience. There was a French pilot who had an artificial arm and when he took off on a sortie, he had to have his arm screwed to the controls. Unfortunately, this pilot crashed in Scotland but was unable to bale out as his arm was fixed to the controls. My husband went to the enquiry and I have never seen him so upset.

After the facts were examined, it appeared that there had been a defect that caused the wings to fall off. The French pilot is buried at Corstphine Hill Cemetery.

My husband, who was called Archie by the boys died last year. I only wish, he were alive to read your book, I most certainly will.

Yours sincerely
Helen Archibald.